www . canadapost . ca .
www . purolator . com .

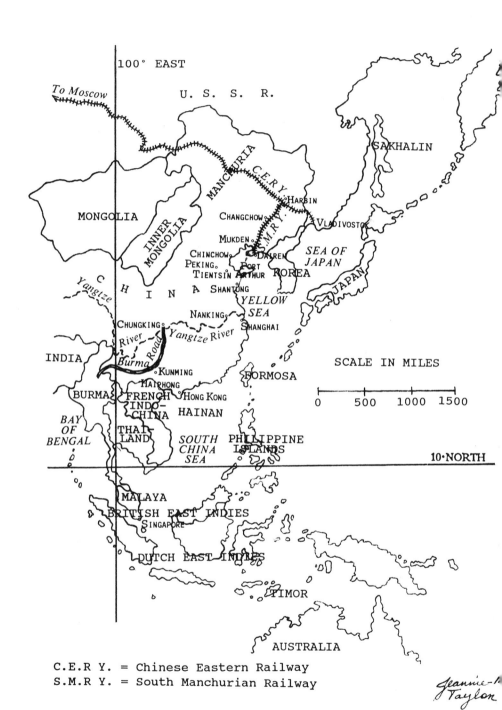

100° EAST

To Moscow

U. S. S. R.

SAKHALIN

MANCHURIA

C.E.R.Y.

HARBIN

MONGOLIA

INNER MONGOLIA

CHANGCHOW

VLADIVOSTOK

MUKDEN

S.M.R.Y.

CHINCHOW

DAIREN

SEA OF JAPAN

PEKING

PORT ARTHUR

KOREA

TIENTSIN

SHANTUNG

JAPAN

Yangtze

C H I N A

YELLOW SEA

NANKING

SEA

CHUNGKING

SHANGHAI

River *Yangtze River*

Burma Road

INDIA

KUNMING

FORMOSA

HAIPHONG

BURMA

FRENCH INDO-CHINA

HONG KONG

HAINAN

SCALE IN MILES

BAY OF BENGAL

THAILAND

SOUTH CHINA SEA

PHILIPPINE ISLANDS

0   500   1000   1500

10·NORTH

MALAYA

BRITISH EAST INDIES

SINGAPORE

DUTCH EAST INDIES

TIMOR

AUSTRALIA

C.E.R Y. = Chinese Eastern Railway
S.M.R Y. = South Manchurian Railway

Jeannie-M
Taylor

TOWARD PEARL HARBOR

The Diplomatic Exchange
Between
Japan and the United States

1899 – 1941

Edited by

Ralph E. Shaffer

California State Polytechnic University
Pomona, California

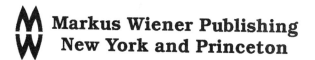 **Markus Wiener Publishing**
New York and Princeton

For information write to:
Markus Wiener Publishing, Inc.
114 Jefferson Road, Princeton, NJ 08540

Library of Congress Cataloging-in-Publication Data

Toward Pearl Harbor: The Diplomatic Exchange Between Japan
and the United States, 1899–1941
Ralph E. Shaffer, ed.

Includes bibliographical references.
1. United States—Foreign Relations—Japan—Sources.   2. Japan—
Foreign Relations—United States—Sources.   3. World War, 1939–
1945—Diplomatic History—Sources.   4. World War,
1939–1945—Causes—Sources.
I. Shaffer, Ralph E.
E183.8.J3T67   1991   327.52073—dc20
91-32081   71980
ISBN 1-55876-046-6
ISBN 1-55876-045-8 (pbk.)

Printed in the United States of America

CONTENTS

INTRODUCTION

To most Americans in December, 1941, the entry of the United States into World War II was very easily explained. In the words of their President:

> Yesterday, December 7, 1941—a date which will live in infamy—the United States of America was suddenly and deliberately attacked by naval and air forces of the Empire of Japan.
>
> The United States was at peace with that nation and, at the solicitation of Japan, was still in conversation with its government and its Emperor looking toward the maintenance of peace in the Pacific. Indeed, one hour after Japanese air squadrons had commenced bombing in Oahu, the Japanese Ambassador to the United States and his colleague delivered to the Secretary of State a formal reply to a recent American message. While this reply stated that it seemed useless to continue the existing diplomatic negotiations, it contained no threat or hint of war or armed attack.
>
> It will be recorded that the distance of Hawaii from Japan makes it obvious that the attack was deliberately planned many days or even weeks ago. During the intervening time the Japanese Government has deliberately sought to deceive the United States by false statements and expressions of hope for continued peace. . . .
>
> The facts of yesterday speak for themselves. The people of the United States have already formed their opinions and well understand the implications to the very life and safety of our nation. . . .

As President Franklin Roosevelt noted, the people had formed their opinions. Simply, it was a case of international bandits (the Axis) engaged in criminal acts. Few Americans cared to challenge this interpretation for to do so would have been to question, during time of war, whether the enormous sacrifice about to be made was really necessary. A negative answer, under those conditions, was unthinkable. But beyond that, few believed that this interpretation was in fact wrong.

Americans looked back upon Japan's action in the Far East during the 1930s and the early 1940s as proof of that nation's aggressive tendencies. Japan could not be trusted to keep her word, as evidenced by her disregard for treaties such as those agreed to at Washington in 1921–1922. Japan was not willing to abide by the principles of international cooperation; witness her withdrawal from the League of Nations. Japan desired to establish economic hegemony in China at the expense of the United States, for how else could Japan's proposed peace terms for China be interpreted? Without question, Japan's motivation was of the most uncivilized nature, designed to exploit her neighbors through intimidation or actual military intervention. Foreign policy was only a means to achieve this end, to be used as a front to conceal military preparations when diplomacy alone would not be sufficient. Or so most Americans believed in the days following Pearl Harbor.

Americans of a later generation, however, less naive about the actions of their own government and seeking to find the basic causes of the conflict as a means of understanding the events of the postwar world, are less likely to accept such a pat explanation. They look instead for causes in basically irreconcilable differences in American and Japanese diplomatic goals. The documents that follow, some of which were unavailable to the public in 1941, put the Japanese government in a more favorable position than previously.

It is now clear that Japanese actions prior to the bombing of Pearl Harbor were motivated by an expected clash of interests with the United States. Japan's foreign policy goals, as developed in the 1930s, were directed toward creation of a Japanese sphere of influence throughout much of Eastern Asia and the Pacific. Japanese diplomats considered this to be in the tradition of European and American foreign policy, and could not understand western opposition to their program.

Japanese statesmen looked upon the treaties of the 1920s as a device by which Europe and America could maintain domination of Asia and frustrate Japanese expansion. Tokyo argued that changing conditions in the 1930s had so altered the alignment of forces that it was wrong for the United States to insist on a literal interpretation of those treaties.

Possessed by fear of economic and military encirclement by the ABCD powers (American, British, Chinese, and Dutch), Japan felt obliged to move outward in response to growing cooperation among those nations. As a partial justification for expansion in the Far East, Japanese diplomats cited their fear of "injurious communist activities" in northeastern Asia, a concern that would justify American intervention in that part of the world after 1945. But neither that argument nor any other could sway the United States in 1941, and Japan's leaders concluded that American and Japanese interests were incompatible. The intransigence of American policy and the apparent futility of diplomatic negotiations left no alternative but war.

The selections that follow present the diplomatic conflict between the United States and Japan as found in executive agreements, treaties, diplomatic notes, intercepted messages, and other documents. Material reproduced here covers the major points of friction between the two nations and is intended to support as fully as possible the views of each country.

Since the roots of World War II in the Pacific reach back to the end of the nineteenth century, fundamental documents covering diplomatic relations between Japan and the United States since 1899 have been included. It is impossible to understand the diplomatic correspondence of the 1930s and early 1940s without reference to John Hay's Open Door Notes, to the bilateral agreements such as Lansing-Ishii, or the Washington Conference. Nor can the outbreak of the Pacific war be viewed so provincially that events related to Europe can be ignored. For that reason, Japan's treaties with various European powers have also been included.

In the documents that follow, readers must be careful to look for all possible meanings and to question the sincerity of each statement. Carefully compare the documents, noting not only different wording but differing interpretations of identical wording. In addition to this textual examination, readers should pay particular attention to the justification put forward by each nation in defense of its policies. Above all, readers must attempt to divorce themselves from traditional, nationalistic interpretations of the events related here. Having done this, they may still reach the conclusions previously held regarding the nature of Japanese ambitions in the Pacific. But the emotions of an earlier era ought not to prevent another interpretation if the evidence leads elsewhere.

To those graduate students who helped in the preparation of this material, I am deeply grateful. Special commendation is due Ben Gracy, Diane Liska, and Barbara Rauch, who sought out many of the documents included here. If the publication suffers from a lack of balance or from omission of important material, it is not their fault. That responsibility is mine.

I

"The Great Aberration:" American Involvement in the Far East (1899–1928)

In the exchange of notes between the United States and Japan during the decade preceding the attack on Pearl Harbor, American diplomats frequently reminded Japanese leaders of the pledges that Japan had made regarding China and the renunciation of war. American notes repeatedly referred to the same treaties and agreements that the United States felt Japan had violated by military and economic action on the mainland of Asia. During the 1930s, while the world still had faith in moral suasion as a method of maintaining the peace, diplomatic correspondence was marked by references to the "Nine-Power Treaty," "Kellogg-Briand Pact," and other less prominent agreements.

The well-trained American note writer always included the right mixture of "administrative and territorial integrity," "equality of commercial opportunity," and "obligations voluntarily assumed to refrain from resort to arms," though phrased in different ways. For their part, Japanese diplomats never failed to remind the United States that such terms referred to "inapplicable or outmoded concepts."

As war between the two nations approached, the notes placed less emphasis upon the importance of honoring these historic pledges, but the ideas that had motivated the agreements remained important. Americans might not insist that they be guaranteed economic rights in China because Japan had signed a treaty to that effect, but Americans did insist on those rights by virtue of their country's economic importance in the Far East. Americans might not talk or write as much about the Kellogg-Briand Pact in 1941 as they had done in 1931, but they were just as insistent that Japan refrain from military action in China.

The basic agreements were important as pledges that nations had made, but even more important because these pledges represented fundamental policies of at least some of the nations that were signatory to them. Not every nation signing a given treaty, however, was as interested in the policy enunciated as another signatory might be. Consequently, Japan could agree to the Nine-Power Treaty without as deep a commitment to the principle of the Open Door as that held by the United States.

American interest in Asia predated the writing of the Constitution, but involvement in the Far East greatly increased with the acquisition of the Philippine Islands following the war with Spain in 1898. While the development of an American Empire was defended on many grounds, Henry Cabot Lodge clearly saw the economic benefits to be gained not only directly in the Philippines but indirectly in China as well. The American victory at Manila Bay, he was to argue in supporting annexation of the Philippines, was the factor that caused the other powers to accept the principle of an Open Door.

But the benefits to be gained required a major deviation from historic American foreign policy. Previous American interest in Asia had been of a limited economic nature, with virtually no diplomatic or military involvement. Acquisition of the Philippines, however, presented the United States with the problem of defending its enlarged economic interest in Asia and its new boundaries from powers, particularly Japan, more formidable than those it had faced in the western hemisphere during the nineteenth century. Americans enjoyed the new prestige that came to their nation through acquisition of overseas possessions, but they were unwilling to pay the price necessary to remain aloof from international obligations in the Far East.

Diplomatic historian Samuel Bemis called America's Asian adventure "the great aberration." Acquisition of the Philippines and the pronouncement of an Open Door in China forced the United States to abandon its traditional policy of noninvolvement with European powers in matters outside the American continents. In so doing, the nation became involved in the politics of not only Asia but of Europe as well. American diplomats understood, almost from the time the Philippines were annexed, that the defense of America's colony could not be achieved by the traditional "go-it-alone" method that had been used to carry out United States policy in the western hemisphere. The nation was neither willing nor able to shoulder the burden required to militarily confront Japan. In remarks intended to discourage American involvement in Manchuria, but also applicable to the Philippines and to China, former President Theodore Roosevelt warned his successor that to fight Japan would require an army equal to Germany's and a fleet the size of Britain's.

Such a military buildup did not appeal to American presidents in the early twentieth century. Instead they chose to rely upon international agreements, both of a bilateral and multilateral nature. While these were to be informal in the first two decades, by the 1920s it had become apparent that a more binding commitment was required. This led to development of the "Washington System," a package of multilateral agreements engineered by Republicans in the Harding Administration. Even then the United States was unwilling to pledge itself to any collective security program involving force for the protection of Asian colonies.

Despite the lack of military cooperation to curtail aggression, prospects for continued peace had brightened by the end of the 1920s. War had been outlawed, China was guaranteed its sovereignty, and open commercial competition seemed assured there. Furthermore, the major nations with Asian interests had pledged themselves to policies that pointed toward a peaceful resolution of problems in the Far East.

The Open Door

From that day in 1785 when their first ship returned from China, American merchants drooled over the prospect of unlimited trade with the world's most populous nation. Throughout the nineteenth century the China trade was never far from the thoughts of businessmen and politicians, who envisioned millions of Chinese constituting a market for American cotton, wheat, timber, and manufactured products. "Oil for the lamps of China" was not an idle phrase.

But other considerations superceded it until the end of the century. In the meantime, European powers dominated China's foreign trade as the major industrial powers vied for its control. By the 1890s there was the distinct possibility that China would go the way of Africa, engulfed by the next episode in the colonial scramble.

The maturing of America's industrial revolution increased interest in trade with the Far East, and events of the 1890s focused that interest on China. The Sino-Japanese War (1894–95), which demonstrated China's weakness, led to a series of European demands that foreshadowed the eventual dismemberment of China. By 1898 several of Europe's major powers had secured spheres of influence in which their nationals had special economic rights. American businessmen faced exclusion from the world's greatest market.

When the Philippines fell to the United States during the Spanish-American War the prospects for American economic activity in China brightened. The physical presence of a powerful navy in the Far East placed American diplomats in a position where they could exert pressure on both China and the other powers to protect American commercial interests in Asia. Traditional American foreign policy precluded a colony on the mainland of Asia, and American businessmen preferred to trade with all of China rather than with a smaller sphere of influence. It was in this context that Secretary of State John Hay sent his Open Door notes to those powers interested in China in 1899.

The United States' Proposal

Mr. Hay to Mr. Buck[1]

Washington, November 13, 1899

This Government, animated with a sincere desire to insure to the commerce and industry of the United States and of all other nations perfect equality of treatment within the limits of the Chinese Empire for their trade and navigation, especially within the so-called "spheres of influence or interest" claimed by certain European powers in China, has deemed the present an opportune moment to make representations in this direction to Germany, Great Britain, and Russia.

To obtain the object it has in view and to remove possible causes of international irritation and reestablish confidence so essential to commerce, it has seemed to this Government highly desirable that the various powers claiming "spheres of interest or influence" in China should give formal assurances that—

First. They will in no way interfere with any treaty port or any vested interest within any so-called "sphere of interest" or leased territory they may have in China.

Second. The Chinese treaty tariff . . . shall apply to all merchandise landed or shipped to all such ports as are within said "sphere of interest" (unless they be "free ports"), no matter to what nationality it may belong, and that duties so leviable shall be collected by the Chinese Government.

Third. They will levy no higher harbor dues on vessels of another nationality frequenting any port in such "sphere" than shall be levied on vessels of their own nationality, and no higher railroad charges over lines built, controlled, or operated within such "sphere" on merchandise belonging to citizens or subjects of other nationalities transported through such "sphere" than shall be levied on similar merchandise belonging to their own nationals transported over equal distances.

The policy pursued by His Imperial German Majesty in declaring Tsing-tao (Kiao-chao) a free port and in aiding the Chinese Government in establishing there a custom-house, and the ukase of His Imperial Russian Majesty of August 11 last in erecting a free port at Dalny (Ta-lien-wan) are thought to be proof that these powers are not disposed to view unfavorably the proposition to recognize that they contemplate nothing which will interfere in any way with the enjoyment by the commerce of all nations of the rights and privileges guaranteed to them by existing treaties with China.

Repeated assurances from the British Government of its fixed policy to maintain throughout China freedom of trade for the whole world insure, it is believed, the ready assent of that power to our proposals. It is no less confidently believed that the commercial interests of Japan would be greatly served by the above-mentioned declaration, which harmonizes with the assurances conveyed to this Government at various times by His Imperial Japanese Majesty's diplomatic representative at this capital.

You [Buck was the American envoy in Japan] are therefore instructed to submit to His Imperial Japanese Majesty's Government the above considerations, and to invite their early attention to them, and express the earnest hope of your Government that they will accept them and aid in securing their acceptance by the other interested powers.

John Hay

Japan's Reply

Viscount Aoki to Mr. Buck[2]

Tokyo, December 26, 1899

Mr. Minister: I have the honor to acknowledge the receipt of [your] note . . . in which, pursuing the instructions of the United States Government, your excellency was so good as to communicate to the Imperial Government the representations of the United States as presented in notes to Russia, Germany, and Great Britain on the subject of commercial interests of the United States in China.

I have the happy duty of assuring your excellency that the Imperial Government will have no hesitation to give their assent to so just and fair a proposal of the United States, provided that all the other powers concerned shall accept the same.

Viscount Siuzo Aoki
Minister for Foreign Affairs

The Open Door: 1900

The European response to Hay's Open Door proposal was highly qualified, as was that of Japan, but early in 1900 Hay announced that all the powers had accepted. The response by some Chinese to what they saw as continued foreign domination of their country came in the form of a popular uprising, known as the Boxer Rebellion, against foreign exploitation of China. When the Chinese government was unable to protect foreign nationals and legations, half a dozen countries, including the United States and Japan, sent troops into China.

Fearful that the incident would be used by some of the intervening powers to further their territorial designs on China, Hay now broadened the Open Door beyond the original concept of commercial equality. The note he sent to the representatives of the United States at Berlin, London, Paris, Rome, St. Petersburg, and Tokyo in July 1900, called for the powers to respect China's territorial integrity and independence. Again, a grudging, half-hearted acceptance marked their response, but for now the fear that China would be divided between Japan and Europe was lessened.

To the Representatives of the United States at Berlin, London, Paris, Rome, St. Petersburg, and Tokyo[3]

Washington, July 3, 1900

In this critical posture of affairs in China it is deemed appropriate to define the attitude of the United States as far as present circumstances permit this to be done. We adhere to the policy initiated by us in 1857, of peace with the Chinese nation, of furtherance of lawful commerce, and of promotion of lives and property of our citizens by all means guaranteed under extraterritorial treaty rights and by the law of nations. If wrong be done to our citizens we propose to hold the responsible authors to the uttermost accountability. We regard the condition at Pekin as one of virtual anarchy, whereby power and responsibility are practically devolved upon the local provincial authorities. So long as they are not in overt collusion with rebellion and use their power to protect foreign life and property we regard them as representing the Chinese people, with whom we seek to remain in peace and friendship. The purpose of the President is, as it has been heretofore, to act concurrently with the other powers, first in opening up communication with Pekin and rescuing the American officials, missionaries, and other Americans who are in danger; secondly, in affording all possible protection everywhere in China to American life and property; thirdly, in guarding and protecting all legitimate American interests; and fourthly, in aiding to prevent a spread of the disorders to the other provinces of the Empire and a recurrence of such disasters. It is, of course, too early to forecast the means of attaining this last result; but the policy of the Government of the United States is to seek a solution which may bring about permanent safety and peace to China, preserve Chinese territorial and administrative entity, protect all rights guaranteed to friendly powers by treaty and international law, and safeguard for the world the principle of equal and impartial trade with all parts of the Chinese Empire.

You will communicate the purport of this instruction to the minister for foreign affairs.

Hay

Bilateral Arrangements With Japan

The Russo-Japanese War (1904–05) changed dramatically the alignment of power in the Far East. Before that conflict, tsarist Russia had been viewed by expansionists as the main danger to American interests in China, threatening to envelop that country in "the darkness of a Russian winter," in the words of Henry Cabot Lodge.

Russia, however, had not been an immediate threat to the Philippines, and, in the euphoria that followed a relatively easy conquest of those islands, their defense was not considered to be a major concern. But Japan's devastating victory on land and sea left the Open Door policy and the Philippines at the mercy of Japan. With Japan militarily supreme in Eastern Asia, and the United States unable or unwilling to match Japanese armed strength, American presidents were forced to rely heavily on diplomacy to protect the nation's interests in Asia.

Initially, America attempted to maintain Japan's good will through bilateral concessions designed to appease Japan by recognizing special Japanese rights in Korea and parts of China. In return, the Japanese gave notice that they would respect America's interests in the Philippines and would honor the Open Door.

In the first of these arrangements, the Taft-Katsura Agreement of 1905, the United States quickly recognized Japanese authority over Korea. That country had been a pawn in the Russo-Japanese War, after which Japan made it a virtual colony. While on a trip to the Far East in 1905, Secretary of War William Howard Taft stopped off in Tokyo. There he negotiated a secret, informal agreement with Count Taro Katsura, Japan's Prime Minister, accepting Japanese hegemony over Korea. In return, Japan honored American control of the Philippines.

By 1908, with relations between the United States and Japan already at the boiling point over Japanese immigration to America and a school discrimination problem in San Francisco, the Open Door was jeopardized by Japanese activity in Manchuria. Russia's defeat had left Japan dominant in Manchuria, which as a Chinese province was covered by the Open Door policy. Unable to force Japan to honor the Open Door in Manchuria, and hopeful that Japanese economic expansion might be contained by compromise, Theodore Roosevelt moved diplomatically to protect American interests. In 1908 Secretary of State Elihu Root and Japan's Ambassador Kogoro Takahira reached a settlement that seemed to accomplish American goals.

The Japanese Ambassador to the Secretary of State [4]

Washington, November 30, 1908

Sir: The exchange of views between us, which has taken place at the several interviews which I have recently had the honor of holding with you, has shown that Japan and the United States holding important outlying insular possessions in the region of the Pacific Ocean, the Governments of the two countries are animated by a common aim, policy, and intention in that region.

Believing that a frank avowal of that aim, policy, and intention would not only tend to strengthen the relations of friendship and good neighborhood, which have immemorially existed between Japan and the United States, but would materially contribute to the preservation of the general peace, the Imperial Government have authorized me to present to you an outline of their understanding of that common aim, policy, and intention:

1. It is the wish of the two Governments to encourage the free and peaceful development of their commerce on the Pacific Ocean.
2. The policy of both Governments, uninfluenced by any aggressive tendencies, is directed to the maintenance of the existing status quo in the region above mentioned and to the defense of the principle of equal opportunity for commerce and industry in China.
3. They are accordingly firmly resolved reciprocally to respect the territorial possessions belonging to each other in said region.
4. They are also determined to preserve the common interest of all powers in China by supporting by all pacific means at their disposal the independence and integrity of China and the principle of equal opportunity for commerce and industry of all nations in that Empire.
5. Should any event occur threatening the status quo as above described or the principle of equal opportunity as above defined, it remains for the two Governments to communicate with each other in order to arrive at an understanding as to what measures they may consider it useful to take.

If the foregoing outline accords with the view of the Government of the United States, I shall be gratified to receive your confirmation.

I take this opportunity to renew to your excellency the assurance of my highest consideration.

K. Takahira

The Secretary of State to the Japanese Ambassador

Washington, November 30, 1908

Excellency: I have the honor to acknowledge the receipt of your note of today setting forth the result of the exchange of views between us in our recent interviews defining the understanding of the two Governments in regard to their policy in the region of the Pacific Ocean.

It is a pleasure to inform you that this expression of mutual understanding is welcome to the Government of the United States as appropriate to the happy relations of the two countries and as the occasion for a concise mutual affirmation of the accordant policy respecting the Far East which the two Governments have so frequently declared in the past.

I am happy to be able to confirm to your excellency, on behalf of the United States, the declaration of the two Governments embodied in the following words:

[The five points made by Takahira were repeated here.]

Accept, Excellency, the renewed assurance of my highest consideration.

Elihu Root

The Lansing-Ishii Agreement

In the midst of World War I, with neither the United States nor any of the European powers in a position to prevent Japanese encroachment on the territory or economy of China, President Woodrow Wilson was forced to enter into bilateral negotiations. Following the pattern of diplomatic concessions already established by Theodore Roosevelt, the Wilson Administration tried to keep ajar an Open Door that Japan had been closing for a decade.

Japan, as an Allied power, occupied German holdings in China early in the war. In 1915 the Japanese government pressed upon China twenty-one economic and territorial demands that would have given Japan domination over much of China. Included in the list were provisions whereby Japan would gain considerable influence in shaping China's domestic policies. Chinese compliance would mean the end of an Open Door.

The initial American response to the Twenty-one Demands was one of opposition, but the European war, even though the United States was neutral, took precedence. Japan withdrew many of the demands as a result of American and British opposition, but, when the United States entered the war in 1917, Wilson found it necessary to reach an understanding with the Japanese.

In November, 1917, Secretary of State Robert Lansing and Japanese Ambassador Kikujiro Ishii exchanged notes containing identical language. The United States conceded to Japan that geographic location made for special relationships, a point that Japan would continue to press in the 1930s and 1940s. Inasmuch as the United States had claimed similar geographic rights in the western hemisphere through the Monroe Doctrine, and had enforced those rights in Cuba through the Platt Amendment and elsewhere in the Caribbean with the Roosevelt Corollary, Japan's demand that geographical propinquity entitled her to a pre-eminent position in the Far East was strengthened.

In addition to the published agreement, there was a secret protocol that was not released until the late 1930s. The terms of the Lansing-Ishii Agreement reveal that it was one more effort to maintain the good will of Japan through additional American concessions that asked of Japan only that it reassert its adherence to already established policy.

The Twenty-one Demands

The Chinese Minister to the Secretary of State[5]

[About February 19, 1915]

Article I

Proposed for the Purpose of Preserving Peace in the Far East and Strengthening the Friendly Relations between the Two Countries

1. China shall recognize the transfer of all the rights in Shantung acquired and enjoyed by Germany in accordance with treaty stipulations or other rights with reference to China, regarding which Japan expects to come to an agreement with Germany eventually.
2. China shall not lease to other countries any territory or island on the coast of Shantung.
3. China shall grant to Japan the right to construct a railway from Yentai or Lungkow to connect with the Kiaochow-Tsinan line.
4. China shall open without delay the principal important cities of Shantung to trade.

Article II

Proposed for the Purpose of Securing to Japan a Position of Special Dominance in South Manchuria and East Mongolia

1. The lease of Port Arthur and Dairen, together with the South Manchurian Railway and the Mukden-Antung Railway, shall be extended to ninety-nine (99) years.
2. Japanese subjects shall have the right to rent and purchase land in South Manchuria and East Mongolia for uses connected with manufactures or agriculture.
3. Japanese subjects shall have the right to go freely to South Manchuria and East Mongolia for purposes of residence and trade.
4. The right to open and operate mines in South Manchuria and East Mongolia shall be granted to Japanese subjects.

5. China shall obtain the consent of the Japanese Government to actions of the two following kinds:
   a. Permitting citizens or subjects of other countries to build railroads in South Manchuria or East Mongolia, or negotiating for loans.
   b. Hypothecating the various revenues of South Manchuria and East Mongolia as security for foreign loans.
6. China shall consult Japan before employing advisers or instructors for conducting the administrative, financial or military affairs of South Manchuria and East Mongolia.
7. Japan shall have control of the Kirin-Changchun railway for ninety-nine (99) years.

Article III

1. China and Japan shall agree to act jointly, not independently, in the contemplated formation of the Han-Yeh-Ping Company.
2. Without consent foreigners shall not be permitted to open and operate mines in the neighborhood of the Han-Yeh-Ping Company's property; and anything affecting the company directly or indirectly shall be decided jointly.

Article IV
Proposed for the Purpose of Effectively Protecting the Territorial Integrity of China

1. China shall not alienate or lease to other countries any port, harbor, or island on the coast of China.

Article V

1. The Central Government of China shall employ influential Japanese subjects as advisers for conducting administrative, financial and military affairs.
2. Japanese hospitals, missions, and schools established in the interior shall have the right to hold land in China.
3. China and Japan shall jointly police the important places in China, or employ a majority of Japanese in the police department of China.
4. China shall purchase from Japan at least half the arms and ammunitions used in the whole country or establish jointly in Japan factories for the manufacture of arms.
5. China shall permit Japan to build railroads connecting Wu Chang with Kiukiang and Nanchang, Nanchang with Hangchow, and Nanchang with Chiaochow (Swatow).
6. In case the Province of Fukien requires foreign capital for railway construction, mining, harbor improvements and shipbuilding Japan shall be first consulted.
7. Japan shall have the right to propagate religious doctrines in China.

The Lansing-Ishii Agreement

The Secretary of State to the Japanese Ambassador on Special Mission[6]

Washington, November 2, 1917

Excellency: I have the honor to communicate herein my understanding of the agreement reached by us in our recent conversations touching the questions of mutual interest to our Governments relating to the Republic of China.

In order to silence mischievous reports that have from time to time been circulated, it is believed by us that a public announcement once more of the desire and intentions shared by our two Governments with regard to China is advisable.

The Governments of the United States and Japan recognize that territorial propinquity creates special relations between countries, and, consequently, the Government of the United States recognizes that Japan has special interests in China, particularly in the part to which her possessions are contiguous.

The territorial sovereignty of China, nevertheless, remains unimpaired and the Government of the United States has every confidence in the repeated assurances of the Imperial Japanese Government that while geographical position gives Japan such special interests they have no desire to discriminate against the trade of other nations or to disregard the commercial rights heretofore granted by China in treaties with other powers.

The Governments of the United States and Japan deny that they have any purpose to infringe in any way the independence or territorial integrity of China and they declare, furthermore, that they always adhere to the principle of the so-called "open door" or equal opportunity for commerce and industry in China.

Moreover, they mutually declare that they are opposed to the acquisition by any Government of any special rights or privileges that would affect the independence or territorial integrity of China or that would deny to the subjects or citizens of any country the full enjoyment of equal opportunity in the commerce and industry of China.

I shall be glad to have your excellency confirm this understanding of the agreement reached by us.

Robert Lansing

Statement by Japanese Ambassador Ishii[7]

Washington, November 2, 1917

Sir: I have the honor to acknowledge the receipt of your note of today, communicating to me your understanding of the agreement reached by us in our recent conversations touching the questions of mutual interest to our Governments relating to the Republic of China.

I am happy to be able to confirm to you, under authorization of my Government, the understanding in question set forth in the follow terms:

[The Japanese reply repeated, without change, all the points contained in Lansing's Nov. 2 note.]

K. Ishii

Secret Protocol [8]

Protocol

In the course of the conversations between the Japanese Special Ambassador and the Secretary of State of the United States which have led to the exchange of notes between them dated this day, declaring the policy of the two Governments with regard to China, the question of embodying the following clause in such declaration came up for discussion: "they (the Governments of Japan and the United States) will not take advantage of the present conditions to seek special rights or privileges in China which would abridge the rights of the subjects or citizens of other friendly states."

Upon careful examination of the question, it was agreed that the clause above quoted being superfluous in the relations of the two Governments and liable to create [an] erroneous impression in the minds of the public, should be eliminated from the declaration.

It was, however, well understood that the principle enunciated in the clause which was thus suppressed was in perfect accord with the declared policy of the two Governments in regard to China.

The Washington Conference and International Cooperation

Disagreements among the victorious powers at the Versailles Conference following World War I increased tension between Japan and the United States. Trouble arose over Japanese rights in China's Shantung peninsula (resolved in favor of Japan) and the failure of the United States to support a Japanese effort to get a clause on racial equality written into the League of Nations Covenant. In addition, there was lingering friction over Japanese intervention in Siberia. With Britain still linked to Japan in a military alliance, American diplomats feared that, should war erupt in the Far East, the United States would face a formidable threat.

Republican presidential candidate Warren Harding promised the American people a return to normalcy if elected in 1920, vowing to seek a more traditional foreign policy in which the nation concentrated on issues of direct concern to the United States. While this was interpreted by much of the public as a return to isolationism, the Harding Administration recognized that twentieth century America, with a highly industrialized economy, could not follow a foreign policy geared to the agrarian days of Jefferson and Jackson.

Even in the neo-isolation of the 1920s the nation had to contend with the problems of the Far East. Conservative presidents were as devoted to the Open Door as their progressive counterparts, Roosevelt and Wilson, had been. Consequently, the Harding Administration could not dispose of Asian problems as easily as it did the question of membership in the League. Instead, Harding and Secretary of State Charles Evans Hughes took the lead in calling a major conference to deal primarily with Pacific area problems. The Washington Conference of 1921–22 was one of the few significant accomplishments of the Harding years.

Three major agreements were reached at Washington, forming the basis for what would later be referred to as the "Washington System." The Four-Power Treaty was designed to encourage consultation among the major Pacific powers in the event that a controversy arose that might endanger peace in the area. It pointedly did not call for collective action, a policy that would have been contrary to the views of most Americans in the 1920s, and it terminated the alliance between Britain and Japan, thereby removing a major threat to American interests.

A second pact, the Five-Power Treaty, limited naval construction in an effort to prevent an anticipated naval armaments race in the 1920s and saved the signatory powers several billion dollars during the next decade. That agreement also restricted further military buildup in various outlying Pacific possessions of the participants, including Guam and the Philippines. With significant modifications that treaty would be renewed at London in 1931.

Some elements in Japan were outraged by an agreement that placed Japan in an inferior naval position vis-a-vis Britain and the United States. The treaty set a ratio that limited Japan to a fleet ⅗ the size of her rivals. That bothered Japanese nationalists, who saw it as another sign of European discrimination against an Asian power. Inasmuch as Japan's naval activity was almost solely confined to the Western Pacific, while Britain and America had world-wide interests, the 5-5-3 ratio in fact left Japan in a position of superiority in the Far East.

The third major treaty consummated at Washington wrote the Open Door into a formal agreement for the first time. The Nine-Power Treaty was ratified by all nations with an interest in China except the Soviet Union, which was not a participant in the conference. Subsequently Japan would withdraw from the Shantung peninsula and would agree to abrogation of the Lansing-Ishii Agreement, both actions seemingly in harmony with the Open Door and the Nine-Power Treaty. Harding and Hughes had apparently accomplished what Roosevelt and Wilson had been unable to do and without making the major concessions that the earlier presidents had found necessary.

The success of the Washington Conference was partly due to the temporary dominance in Japan of a democratic tendency in the 1920s. The civil government had fallen into the hands of moderates who sought to pursue Japan's interest through diplomacy rather than military conquest. The subordination of the military, however, was momentary and by the end of the 1920s the future of a western-style parliamentary system in Japan was in doubt. The military, especially that part of it that was committed to expansion in East Asia, would regain influence in shaping the nation's foreign policy in the decade before Pearl Harbor.

In the 1930s American diplomats would cite the treaties hammered out at Washington, along with the Kellogg-Briand Pact of 1928, whenever Japan took action that jeopardized peace in the Pacific. In return, Japan, by then heavily influenced by expansionists who saw the treaties of the 1920s as a deterrent to their territorial ambitions, responded that international conditions, particularly in China, had so changed that Japan was no longer obligated to abide by the Washington agreements.

The Four-Power Treaty

Treaty between the United States of America, the British Empire, France, and Japan [9]

Signed at Washington December 13, 1921

The United States of America, the British Empire, France and Japan,

With a view to the preservation of the general peace and the maintenance of their rights in relation to their insular possessions and insular dominions in the region of the Pacific Ocean,

Have determined to conclude a Treaty to this effect and have . . . agreed as follows:

I

The High Contracting parties agree . . . to respect their rights in relation to their insular possessions and insular dominions in the region of the Pacific Ocean.

If there should develop between any of the High Contracting Parties a controversy arising out of any Pacific question and involving their said rights which is not satisfactorily settled by diplomacy and is likely to affect the harmonious accord now happily subsisting between them, they shall invite the other High Contracting Parties to a joint conference to which the whole subject will be referred for consideration and adjustment.

II

If the said rights are threatened by the aggressive action of any other power, the High Contracting Parties shall communicate with one another fully and frankly in order to arrive at an understanding as to the most efficient measures to be taken, jointly or separately, to meet the exigencies of the particular situation.

III

This Treaty shall remain in force for ten years from the time it shall take effect, and after the expiration of said period it shall continue to be in force subject to the right of any of the High Contracting Parties to terminate it upon twelve months' notice.

IV

This Treaty shall be ratified as soon as possible . . . and thereupon the agreement between Great Britain and Japan, which was concluded at London on July 13, 1911, shall terminate. . . .

Supplementary Declaration, Signed December 13, 1921

In signing the Treaty this day between The United States of America, The British Empire, France and Japan, it is declared to be the understanding and intent of the Signatory Powers:

1. That the Treaty shall apply to the Mandated Islands in the Pacific Ocean; provided, however, that the making of the Treaty shall not be deemed to be an assent on the part of The United States of America to the mandates and shall not preclude agreements between The United States of America and the Mandatory Powers respectively in relation to the mandated islands.

2. That the controversies to which the second paragraph of Article I refers shall not be taken to embrace questions which according to prin-

ciples of international law lie exclusively within the domestic jurisdiction of the respective powers.

Agreement between the United States of America, the British Empire, France and Japan, Supplementary to the Treaty of December 13, 1921, Signed at Washington February 6, 1922

The United States of America, the British Empire, France and Japan have, through their respective Plenipotentiaries, agreed upon the following stipulations supplementary to the Quadruple Treaty signed at Washington on December 13, 1921:

The term "insular possessions and insular dominions" used in the aforementioned Treaty shall, in its application to Japan, include only Karafuto (or the Southern portion of the island of Sakhalin), Formosa and the Pescadores, and the islands under the mandate of Japan.

The present agreement shall have the same force and effect as the said Treaty to which it is supplementary. . . .

The Five-Power Treaty

Treaty between the United States of America, the British Empire, France, Italy, and Japan [10]

Signed at Washington February 6, 1922

The United States of America, the British Empire, France, Italy and Japan;
    Desiring to contribute to the maintenance of the general peace, and to reduce the burdens of competition in armament;
    . . . have agreed as follows:

Article I
The Contracting Powers agree to limit their respective naval armament as provided in the present Treaty. . . .

Article IV
The total capital ship replacement tonnage of each of the Contracting Powers shall not exceed in standard displacement, for the United States 525,000 tons; for the British Empire 525,000 tons; for France 175,000 tons; for Italy 175,000 tons; for Japan 315,000 tons.

Article V
No capital ship exceeding 35,000 tons standard displacement shall be acquired by, or constructed by, for, or within the jurisdiction of, any of the Contracting Powers.

Article VI

No capital ship of any of the Contracting Powers shall carry a gun with a calibre in excess of 16 inches.

Article VII

The total tonnage for aircraft carriers of each of the Contracting Powers shall not exceed in standard displacement, for the United States 135,000 tons; for the British Empire, 135,000 tons; for France 60,000 tons; for Italy 60,000 tons; for Japan 81,000 tons. . . .

Article XII

No vessel of war of any of the Contracting Powers, hereafter laid down, other than a capital ship, shall carry a gun with a calibre in excess of 8 inches. . . .

Article XIX

The United States, the British Empire and Japan agree that the *status quo* at the time of the signing of the present Treaty, with regard to fortifications and naval bases, shall be maintained in their respective territories and possessions specified hereunder:

1. The insular possessions which the United States now holds or may hereafter acquire in the Pacific Ocean, except (a) those adjacent to the coast of the United States, Alaska and the Panama Canal Zone, not including the Aleutian Islands, and (b) the Hawaiian islands;
2. Hongkong and the insular possessions which the British Empire now holds or may hereafter acquire in the Pacific Ocean, east of the meridian of 110° east longitude, except (a) those adjacent to the coast of Canada, (b) the Commonwealth of Australia and its Territories, and (c) New Zealand;
3. The following insular territories and possessions of Japan in the Pacific Ocean, to wit: the Kurile Islands, the Bonin Islands, Amami-Oshima, the Loochoo Islands, Formosa and the Pescadores, and any insular territories or possessions in the Pacific Ocean which Japan may hereafter acquire.

The maintenance of the *status quo* under the foregoing provisions implies that no new fortifications or naval bases shall be established in the territories and possessions specified; that no measures shall be taken to increase the existing naval facilities for the repair and maintenance of naval forces, and that no increase shall be made in the coast defences of the territories and possessions above specified. This restriction, however, does not preclude such repair and replacement of worn-out weapons and equipment as is customary in naval and military establishments in time of peace. . . .

Rules for Replacement

. . . No capital ship . . . [there were minor, very specific exceptions] shall be laid down until ten years from November 12, 1921. . . .

Definitions
A capital ship . . . is defined as a vessel of war, not an aircraft carrier, whose displacement exceeds 10,000 tons . . . or which carries a gun with a calibre exceeding 8 inches. . . .

Article XXIII
The present Treaty shall remain in force until December 31st, 1936, and in case none of the Contracting Powers shall have given notice two years before that date of its intention to terminate the Treaty, it shall continue in force until the expiration of two years from the date on which notice of termination shall be given by one of the Contracting Powers, whereupon the Treaty shall terminate as regards all the Contracting Powers. . . .

Nine-Power Treaty

Treaty between the United States of America, Belgium, the British Empire, China, France, Italy, Japan, the Netherlands, and Portugal[11]

Signed at Washington February 6, 1922

The [Contracting Powers]:
Desiring to adopt a policy designed to stabilize conditions in the Far East, to safeguard the rights and interests of China, and to promote intercourse between China and the other Powers upon the basis of equality of opportunity; . . .
Have resolved to conclude a treaty for that purpose. . . .

Article I
The Contracting Powers, other than China, agree:
1. To respect the sovereignty, the independence, and the territorial and administrative integrity of China;
2. To provide the fullest and most unembarrassed opportunity to China to develop and maintain for herself an effective and stable government;
3. To use their influence for the purpose of effectually establishing and maintaining the principle of equal opportunity for the commerce and industry of all nations throughout the territory of China;
4. To refrain from taking advantage of conditions in China in order to seek special rights or privileges which would abridge the rights of subjects or citizens of friendly States, and from countenancing action inimical to the security of such States.

Article II
The Contracting Powers agree not to enter into any treaty, agreement, arrangement, or understanding, either with one another, or, individually

or collectively, with any Power of Powers, which would infringe or impair the principles stated in Article I.

Article III

With a view to applying more effectually the principles of the Open Door or equality of opportunity in China for the trade and industry of all nations, the Contracting Powers, other than China, agree that they will not seek, nor support their respective nationals in seeking—

a. any arrangement which might purport to establish in favour of their interests any general superiority of rights with respect to commercial or economic development in any designated region of China;

b. any such monopoly or preference as would deprive the nationals of any other Power of the right of undertaking any legitimate trade or industry in China, or of participating with the Chinese Government, or with any local authority, in any category of public enterprise, or which by reason of its scope, duration or geographical extent is calculated to frustrate the practical application of the principle of equal opportunity.

It is understood that the foregoing stipulations of this Article are not to be so construed as to prohibit the acquisition of such properties or rights as may be necessary to the conduct of a particular commercial, industrial, or financial undertaking or to the encouragement of invention and research.

China undertakes to be guided by the principles stated in the foregoing stipulations of this Article in dealing with applications for economic rights and privileges from Governments and nationals of all foreign countries, whether parties to the present Treaty or not.

Article IV

The Contracting Powers agree not to support any agreements by their respective nationals with each other designed to create Spheres of Influence or to provide for the enjoyment of mutually exclusive opportunities in designated parts of Chinese territory.

Article V

China agrees that, throughout the whole of the railways in China, she will not exercise or permit unfair discrimination of any kind. In particular there shall be no discrimination whatever, direct or indirect, in respect of charges or of facilities on the ground of the nationality of passengers or the countries from which or to which they are proceeding, or the origin or ownership of goods or the country from which or to which they are consigned, or the nationality or ownership of the ship or other means of conveying such passengers or goods before or after their transport on the Chinese Railways.

The Contracting Powers, other than China, assume a corresponding obligation in respect of any of the aforesaid railways over which they or their nationals are in a position to exercise any control in virtue of any concession, special agreement or otherwise.

Article VI

The Contracting Powers, other than China, agree fully to respect China's rights as a neutral in time of war to which China is not a party; and China declares that when she is a neutral she will observe the obligations of neutrality.

Article VII

The Contracting Powers agree that, whenever a situation arises which in the opinion of any one of them involves the application of the stipulations of the present Treaty, and renders desirable discussion of such application, there shall be full and frank communication between the Contracting Powers concerned.

Article VIII

Powers not signatory to the present Treaty, which have Governments recognized by the Signatory Powers and which have treaty relations with China, shall be invited to adhere to the present Treaty. To this end the Government of the United States will make the necessary communications to nonsignatory Powers and will inform the Contracting Powers of the replies received. Adherence by any Power shall become effective on receipt of notice thereof by the Government of the United States. . . .

"Outlawing War": The Kellogg-Briand Pact

Implementation of Republican foreign policy in the 1920s centered on moral suasion, a view that war could be prevented more effectively by the force of international public opinion than by the threat of collective military security. This was a concept that fit neatly into a decade that witnessed calls for the "outlawry of war" and a return to normalcy. Its culmination came with adoption of the Kellogg-Briand Pact, or the Pact of Paris, in 1928.

The impetus initially came from France in the form of a proposal by the French Foreign Minister, Aristide Briand, for a treaty between the United States and France renouncing the use of force to settle disputes between the two nations. Skeptics wondered if this was but a forerunner of an attempt to revive the unratified collective security agreement that Wilson had negotiated with the French at the end of World War I.

But the idea of renouncing war as an instrument of resolving international disputes was a popular idea. Secretary of State Frank Kellogg therefore broadened the proposal for a bilateral treaty into an open-ended agreement that any nation could support. In 1928 a handful of governments initially signed the pact. Within a few years nearly every nation in the world would sign, including most of the countries that participated in World War II.

As a signatory power, Japan was rebuked for violating the pact in 1931 when the Japanese army occupied Manchuria and in 1937 when Japan launched an undeclared war on China. The pact would continue to serve as a tool of American diplomacy down to 1941 as Washington diplomats resurrected it to remind the Japanese that they had violated their pledged word. But by then whatever usefulness it may have had in maintaining peace had long since disappeared.

Renunciation of War as an Instrument of National Policy [12]
(Kellogg-Briand Peace Pact or Pact of Paris)

The President of the German Reich, The President of the United States of America, His Majesty the King of The Belgians, the President of The French Republic, His Majesty the King of Great Britain, Ireland and The British Dominions Beyond the Seas, Emperor of India, His Majesty the King of Italy, His Majesty the Emperor of Japan, the President of the Republic of Poland, the President of the Czechoslovak Republic,

Deeply sensible of their solemn duty to promote the welfare of mankind;

Persuaded that the time has come when a frank renunciation of war as an instrument of national policy should be made to the end that the peaceful and friendly relations now existing between their peoples may be perpetuated;

Convinced that all changes in their relations with one another should be sought only by pacific means and be the result of a peaceful and orderly process, and that any signatory Power which shall hereafter seek to promote its national interests by resort to war should be denied the benefits furnished by this Treaty;

Hopeful that, encouraged by their example, all the other nations of the world will join in this humane endeavor and by adhering to the present Treaty as soon as it comes into force bring their peoples within the scope of its beneficent provisions, thus uniting the civilized nations of the world in a common renunciation of war as an instrument of their national policy;

Have decided to conclude a Treaty and for that purpose have . . . agreed upon the following articles:

Article I

The High Contracting Parties solemnly declare in the names of their respective peoples that they condemn recourse to war for the solution of international controversies, and renounce it as an instrument of national policy in their relations with one another.

Article II

The High Contracting Parties agree that the settlement or solution of all disputes or conflicts of whatever nature or of whatever origin they may be, which may arise among them, shall never be sought except by pacific means.

Article III

The present Treaty shall be ratified by the High Contracting Parties named in the Preamble in accordance with their respective constitutional requirements, and shall take effect . . . as soon as all their several instruments of ratification shall have been deposited at Washington.

This Treaty shall, when it has come into effect as prescribed in the preceding paragraph, remain open as long as may be necessary for adherence by all the other Powers of the world. . . .

Done at Paris, [August 27, 1928]. . . .

Notes

1. U. S. Department of State, *Foreign Relations of the United States: 1899* (Washington, 1901), 138–139.

2. *Ibid.*, 139.

3. U. S. Department of State, *Foreign Relations of the United States: 1900* (Washington, 1902), 299.

4. U. S. Department of State, *Foreign Relations of the United States: 1908* (Washington, 1912), 510–512.

5. U. S. Department of State, *Foreign Relations of the United States, 1915* (Washington, 1924), 93–95. This document, purportedly a copy of the demands Japan made on China, was delivered to the Secretary of State by the Chinese Minister in Washington.

6. U. S. Department of State, *Foreign Relations of the United States: 1917* (Washington, 1926), 264.

7. *Ibid.*, 265.

8. U. S. Department of State, *Foreign Relations of the United States: 1922* (Washington, 1938), II, 595.

9. *Ibid.*, I, 33-37, 46.

10. *Ibid.*, I, 247–266.
11. *Ibid.*, I, 276–280.
12. U. S. Department of State, *Treaties and other international agreements of the United States of America: 1776–1949* (Washington, 1969), II, 732–735.

II

THE MANCHURIAN INCIDENT

On September 18, 1931, an explosion of mysterious origin along the tracks of the South Manchurian Railroad near Mukden destroyed the fragile peace agreements painstakingly negotiated over the past two decades. Troops stationed there to protect Japan's interests on the Liaotung peninsula clashed with forces from China, of which Manchuria was nominally a part. Within a year and a half the optimistic view formulated in the 1920s that peace could be maintained by moral suasion would be shattered. Instead, the Manchurian Incident, as it was called, would leave in its wake the wreckage of the Washington treaties, the Kellogg-Briand Pact and the League of Nations, now revealed to be an impotent debating society unable to assert its will effectively.

The incident near Mukden was the culmination of a nearly forty year contest for control of Manchuria between Japan and Russia. At the end of the Sino-Japanese War (1894–95) a victorious Japan had tried to gain control of Manchuria's Liaotung peninsula but was frustrated by a combination of European powers, including Russia. Active Russian interest in the region also began then, as the Russians built the Trans-Siberian Railroad through northern Manchuria to Vladivostok. The portion of the line that crossed northern Manchuria was known as the Chinese Eastern Railway, while a branch to Port Arthur, also constructed by Russia, was called the South Manchurian Railway. During the Boxer Rebellion Russia sent troops into Manchuria, ostensibly to protect Russian nationals and property but at the same time increasing Russian influence there.

Japan was fearful that, with completion of the Trans-Siberian line, tsarist Russia would become a more formidable power in the Far East, particularly in Manchuria (on which Japan still had designs) and would threaten Japanese interests in Korea. When negotiations with Russia over the future of Manchuria bogged down, Japan struck Russian land and sea units in the Far East and won a stunning military and psychological victory, emerging from the Russo-Japanese War (1904–05) as the major power in eastern Asia.

By the Treaty of Portsmouth (1905), brokered by Theodore Roosevelt, Japan gained control of Russian leaseholds in the Kwantung section of southern Manchuria, including Port Arthur and the South Manchurian Railway. Manchuria remained officially Chinese, but over the next quarter century Japanese influence there grew. Japan encouraged its surplus population to migrate there by the thousands, and Japanese businessmen took advantage of the opportunities in this largely undeveloped area.

The Chinese Eastern Railway remained under Russian control, even after the Bolshevik Revolution brought communists to power in Russia. But a strengthened Chinese government, led by Chiang Kai-shek and his Nationalist (Kuomintang) party, seized the railroad in 1929 in an effort to oust Soviet influence in northern Manchuria. The Soviet response was a quick military strike that regained the railroad and reestablished Russian authority in that part of the Chinese province.

Frustrated in northern Manchuria, the Chinese turned toward the Japanese holdings in the south. By 1931 expansionists in Japan were fearful that China would be able, with European and American support, to reassert control in southern Manchuria. Concerned that the civilian government at Tokyo was likely to bow to foreign pressure, military leaders within Japan's Manchuria-based Kwantung Army conspired to create an incident that would give the army an excuse to drive Chinese forces from all of Manchuria, establishing Japanese control of the area without question.

Japan Explains Her Manchurian Action

Late on the night of September 18, 1931, the "Manchurian Incident" began. Nelson Johnson, the American Minister in China, sent a dispatch to Washington at 2:30 a.m. the following morning, citing a secondhand report that Japanese troops had "apparently run amuck" and had fired on Mukden. Japan blamed the outburst on Chinese army units that had destroyed track along the South Manchurian Railway. This explanation was promptly reported to Washington by Minister Johnson who dismissed it as absurd, citing rumors which he had previously discounted that Japan had plans to occupy Manchuria and reports from travellers that Japanese troops had for two or three weeks staged mock assaults in towns along the rail line.

Nearly a week after the fighting began at Mukden, Japan sent a formal message to the State Department, presenting Japan's official explanation of what occurred on September 18.

The Japanese Embassy to the Department of State[1]

Statement Issued After Extraordinary Cabinet Meeting, September 24, 1931.

1. The Japanese Government has constantly been exercising honest endeavors in pursuance of its settled policy to foster friendly relations between Japan and China and to promote the common prosperity and well-being of the two countries. Unfortunately, the conduct of officials and individuals of China, for some years past, has been such that our national sentiment has frequently been irritated. In particular, unpleasant incidents have taken place one after another in regions of Manchuria and Mongolia in which Japan is interested in especial degree until an impression has gained strength in the minds of the Japanese people that Japan's fair and friendly attitude is not being reciprocated by China in like spirit. Amidst an atmosphere of perturbation and anxiety thus created a detachment of Chinese troops destroyed tracks of the South Manchurian Railway in the vicinity of Mukden and attacked our railway guards at midnight of September 18th. A clash between Japanese and Chinese troops then took place.
2. The situation became critical as the number of Japanese guards stationed along the entire railway did not then exceed ten thousand four hundred while there were in juxtaposition some two hundred twenty thousand Chinese soldiers. Moreover, hundreds of thousands of Japanese residents were placed in jeopardy. In order to forestall imminent disaster the Japanese army had to act swiftly. The Chinese soldiers, garrisoned in neighboring localities, were disarmed and the duty of maintaining peace and order was left in the hands of the local Chinese organizations under the supervision of the Japanese troops.
3. These measures having been taken, our soldiers were mostly withdrawn within the railway zone. There still remain some detachments in Mukden and Kirin and [a] small number of men in a few other places. But nowhere does a state of military occupation as such exist.

Reports that Japanese authorities have seized [the] customs . . . office at Yingkou or that they have taken control of Chinese railways . . . are entirely untrue, nor has the story of our troops having ever been sent north of Changchun or into Chientao any foundation in fact.

4. The Japanese Government at a special cabinet meeting September 19th took decision [*sic*] that all possible efforts should be made to prevent aggravation of the situation and instructions to that effect were given to the commander of the Manchurian garrison. It is true that a detachment was despatched from Changchun to Kirin September 21st, but it was not with a view to military occupation but only for the purpose of removing the menace to the South Manchurian Railway on [our] flank. As soon as that object has been attained the bulk of our detachment will be withdrawn. It may be added that while a mixed brigade of four thousand men was sent from Korea to join the Manchurian garrison the total number of men in the garrison at present still remains within the limit set by the treaty and that fact cannot therefore be regarded as having in any way added to the seriousness of the international situation.

5. It may be superfluous to repeat that the Japanese Government harbors no territorial designs in Manchuria. What we desire is that Japanese subjects shall be enabled to safely engage in various peaceful pursuits and be given an opportunity for participating in the development of that land by means of capital and labor. It is the proper duty of a government to protect the rights and interests legitimately enjoyed by the nation or individuals. The endeavors of the Japanese Government to guard the South Manchurian Railway against wanton attacks would be viewed in no other light. The Japanese Government, true to established policy, is prepared to cooperate with the Chinese Government in order to prevent the present incident from developing into a disastrous situation between the two countries and to work out such constructive plans as will once [and] for all eradicate causes for future friction. The Japanese Government would be more than gratified if the present difficulty could be brought to a solution which will give a new turn to mutual relations of the two countries.

Manchuria and the Kellogg Pact

In Washington, Secretary of State Henry L. Stimson met with Japanese Ambassador Katsuji Debuchi on September 22. Stimson opened the conversation by recalling that at their previous meeting on the 17th both of them "expressed our feeling that the relations of our two countries were in such a satisfactory condition." Now, less than a week later, the Manchurian Incident threatened the tenuous balance that had existed in China throughout the 1920s.

Though raising questions about the Kellogg Pact and the Washington treaties, Stimson stopped far short of charging Japan with violation of those agreements. He told Debuchi that the current situation, with Japan in military occupation of south Manchuria, was no doubt embarrassing to the Japanese government, and he professed that American action was designed to strengthen the hand of Baron Shidehara, Japan's Foreign Minister, who apparently was at odds with Japanese military forces in Manchuria. Debuchi agreed that the military and civilian elements in his government were divided by the action in Manchuria.

In the meantime, China had protested to both the United States and the League of Nations, charging Japan with an "unprovoked and unwarranted attack" that had resulted in Japanese occupation of several Chinese cities. The Chinese relied heavily on the Kellogg Pact, hoping that the United States would feel obliged to act in defense of an agreement so closely associated with Republican foreign policy of the 1920s.

Moving with great caution, Stimson sent a proposal for action to Minister Johnson in Peiping on September 24. A month later, after Japan had significantly extended the war into other areas of southern Manchuria, the United States participated in League discussions on the Manchurian question insofar as invocation of the Kellogg Pact was concerned. The League called for Japanese forces to return to the positions they occupied prior to the railway incident and sent a commission, headed by Britain's Lord Lytton and including an American representative, to investigate. Simultaneously, Stimson sent Japan a note reminding the Japanese of their obligations under Kellogg. In reply, the Japanese government suggested that the action in Manchuria was designed to carry out the intent of the Kellogg Pact.

Stimson Proposes a Plan

The Secretary of State to the Minister in China (Johnson)[2]

Washington, September 24, 1931

For your personal information, I want to give you, with regard to your various telegrams concerning the trouble in Manchuria, a picture of the policy of the Department.

The Department, as already reported, is completely sympathetic with the action of sending identic notes to Japan and China already taken by the League of Nations. However, the idea of sending a military commission to Manchuria to establish the facts disturbed us. At the time of the dispute between Bulgaria and Greece this was done by the League with success. Entirely different, however, are the conditions in the Manchurian situation. The issue in the Bulgarian-Greek dispute was a line dividing the two countries. In Manchuria, since the Japanese troops are in that section of China under treaty provisions, no such issue arises. Moreover, even as a fact-finding body, the Department has felt very strongly that a commission sent to Manchuria could have little success without the consent of both the Chinese and Japanese. That the Japanese nationalistic element would be immensely strengthened and that it would unite Japan behind the military element, is our principal fear concerning such an imposed commission. The civilian arm of the Government in Japan, we believe, is opposed to the adventure in Manchuria, and the Department feels it is important in every way to support this element. It was our suggestion to Geneva, therefore, that there was a greater possibility of obtaining the consent of Japan if the composition of the commission to be appointed were to be along the lines of our suggestion of two years ago to China and Russia. In other words, the commission should be one appointed by both parties involved in the dispute. The League has adopted this suggestion and, if Japan accepts, at present intends to establish a commission consisting of two members appointed by Japan, two by China, and three by the League Council. This commission we understand would be purely fact finding and have very narrow terms of reference. However, if it can be brought about between the Japanese and Chinese, we believe there is a much greater chance of reaching a solution—in view of Oriental psychology—by direct consultation. The Department feels at the same time that inevitably the dispute is of interest to the world, and that it would make a travesty of the various treaties of which Japan and China are both signatories to allow Japan to consolidate the occupation of the Manchurian cities. Since in this matter the League has already taken action and since as members of the League both parties have agreed to submit to the action therein provided, this Government would be inclined to favor, in case direct conversations are unsuccessful between the two parties, action under . . . articles of the League Covenant signed by both Japan and China.

The treaties of 1922 and the Kellogg Pact still remain and might be invoked in case this action should be unsuccessful. The above is, in general, the line we intend to take. Any comments or further suggestions you wish to make would be welcomed. . . .

Henry L. Stimson

Stimson Reminds Japan of the Kellogg Pact

The Secretary of State to the Japanese Minister for Foreign Affairs[3]

Washington, October 20, 1931

The Government and people of the United States have observed with concern the events of the last month in Manchuria. When the difference between Japan and China came to a head on September 19th one of the parties to the dispute referred the matter to the League of Nations and since that time the American Government by representations through diplomatic channels, has steadily cooperated with the League in its efforts to secure a peaceful settlement. A threat of war, wherever it may rise, is of profound concern to the whole world and for this reason the American Government, like other Governments, was constrained to call to the attention of both disputants the serious dangers involved in the present situation.

This Government now desires, as do other signatories of the Treaty for the Renunciation of War, particularly to call to the attention of the Japanese and the Chinese Governments the obligations which they voluntarily assumed when they became parties to that Treaty, especially the obligations of Article II. . . .

The American Government takes this occasion again to express its earnest hope that Japan and China will refrain from any measures which might lead to war and that they will find it possible in the near future to agree upon a method for resolving by peaceful means, in accordance with their promises and in keeping with the confident expectations of public opinion throughout the world, the issues over which they are at present in controversy.

Stimson

Japan Reconciles Intervention with Renunciation of War

A Statement by the Japanese Minister for Foreign Affairs[4]

Tokyo, October 24, 1931

1. The Japanese Government realize as fully as any other signatories of the Pact of Paris of 1928, the responsibility incurred under the provisions of that solemn pact. They have made it clear on various occasions that the Japanese railway guards in taking military measures in Manchuria since the night of September 18 last have been actuated solely by the necessity of defending themselves as well as of protecting the South Manchuria Railway and the lives and property of Japanese subjects, against wanton attacks by Chinese troops and armed

bands. Nothing is farther from the thoughts of the Japanese Government than to have recourse to war for the solution of their outstanding differences in China.

2. It is their settled aim to compose those differences by all pacific means. . . . The Japanese Government have already declared their readiness to enter into negotiations with the responsible representatives of China for an adjustment of the present difficulties. They still hold the same view. So far as they are concerned, they have no intention whatever of proceeding to any steps that might hamper any efforts intended to assure the pacific settlement of the conflict between Japan and China.

3. On the other hand they have repeatedly called the attention of the Chinese Government to the organized hostile agitation against Japan now in progress in various parts of China. The suspension of all commercial intercourse with Japanese at present in China is in no sense a spontaneous act of individual Chinese. It is enforced by anti-Japanese organizations that have taken the law into their own hands, and are heavily penalizing, even with the threat of capital punishment, any Chinese who may be found disobeying their arbitrary decrees. Acts of violence leveled against Japanese residents also continue unabated in many places under the jurisdiction of the Government of Nanking. It will be manifest to all fair observers of the actual situation that those activities of the anti-Japanese organizations are acquiesced in by the Chinese Government as a means to attain the national ends of China. The Japanese Government desire to point out that such acquiescence by the Chinese Government in the lawless proceedings of their own nationals cannot be regarded as being in harmony with the letter or the spirit of the stipulations contained in . . . the Pact of Paris.

The Stimson Doctrine

From late 1931 until the end of his term in 1933, the administration of President Herbert Hoover attempted to deal with a worsening Manchurian problem. Mired down in the worst depression yet faced by the United States and committed to moral suasion rather than military action, Hoover found his options in the Far East greatly limited. By nature he shrank from the possible use of force against Japan, preferring some other resolution of the increasingly difficult issue. The nation was militarily unprepared for war in Asia, and Hoover recognized that a bellicose posture might provide the spark for Japanese action far beyond the limited area of Manchuria. This was the age of disillusionment with World War I, and

Americans were not inclined to resort to force in a region so remote and apparently so unimportant. Already criticized for having curtailed American overseas commerce by signing the Smoot-Hawley Tariff, Hoover was unwilling to further dampen foreign trade by imposing an embargo on Japan.

Secretary of State Stimson, more anxious than Hoover to take a firm stand on Manchuria, made one last effort to apply the moral suasion concept that had dominated Republican foreign policy in the 1920s. On January 7, 1932, he sent notes to both China and Japan announcing what has come to be known as the Stimson Doctrine, a policy of nonrecognition of changes brought about in violation of the Kellogg Pact.

The Japanese response was twofold. Diplomatically, Japan again claimed to be maintaining the spirit of the Kellogg Pact. Militarily, Japan flaunted the calls from the League and the United States for a peaceful resolution by extending the war to Shanghai, where fighting broke out in January, raising fears for the safety of a large foreign population there. In frustration, Stimson sent a lengthy letter to Sen. William Borah, Republican isolationist and chairman of the Senate Foreign Relations Committee, in which he painstakingly detailed the evolution of the Open Door policy and the international agreements reached at Washington a decade earlier. The letter, made public by Stimson, was a precise summation of American policy to that time.

Stimson Announces the Doctrine

The Secretary of State to the Ambassador in Japan (Forbes)[5]

Washington, January 7, 1932

Please deliver to the Foreign Office on behalf of your Government as soon as possible the following note:

With the recent military operations about Chinchow, the last remaining administrative authority of the Government of the Chinese Republic in South Manchuria, as it existed prior to September 18th, 1931, has been destroyed. The American Government continues confident that the work of the neutral commission recently authorized by the Council of the League of Nations will facilitate an ultimate solution of the difficulties now existing between China and Japan. But in view of the present situation and of its own rights and obligations therein, the American Government deems it to be its duty to notify both the Imperial Japanese government and the Government of the Chinese Republic that it cannot admit the legality of any situation *de facto* nor does it intend to recognize any treaty or agreement entered into between those Governments, or agents thereof, which may impair the treaty rights of the United States or its citizens in China, including those which relate to the sovereignty, the independence, or the territorial and administrative integrity of the Republic of China, or to the international policy relative to China, commonly known as the open door policy; and that it does not intend to recognize any situation, treaty or agreement which may be brought about by means contrary to the covenants and obligations of the Pact of Paris of August 27, 1928, to which Treaty both China and Japan, as well as the United States, are parties.

Japan Answers Stimson

The Ambassador in Japan (Forbes) to the Secretary of State[6]

Tokyo, January 16, 1932

I have just received the reply of the Japanese Government which reads as follows:

. . . The Government of Japan were well aware that the Government of the United States could always be relied on to do everything in their power to support Japan's efforts to secure the full and complete fulfillment in every detail of the treaties of Washington and the Kellogg Treaty for the Outlawry of War. They are glad to receive this additional assurance of the fact.

As regards the question which Your Excellency specifically mentions of the policy of the so-called 'open door,' the Japanese Government, as has so often been stated, regard that policy as a cardinal feature of the politics of the Far East, and regrets that its effectiveness is so seriously diminished by the unsettled conditions which prevail throughout China. Insofar as they can secure it, the policy of the open door will always be maintained in Manchuria, as in China proper.

They take note of the statement by the Government of the United States that the latter cannot admit the legality of matters which might impair the treaty rights of the United States or its citizens or which might be brought about by means contrary to the [Kellogg-Briand] treaty of 27 August, 1928. It might be the subject of an academic doubt whether in a given case the impropriety of means necessarily and always voids the ends secured; but as Japan has no intention of adopting improper means, that question does not practically arise.

It may be added that the treaties which relate to China must necessarily be applied with due regard to the state of affairs from time to time prevailing in that country, and that the present unsettled and distracted state of China is not what was in the contemplation of the High Contracting Parties at the time of the Treaty of Washington. It was certainly not satisfactory then; but it did not display that disunion and those antagonisms which it does today. This cannot affect the binding character or the stipulations of treaties; but it may in material respects modify their application, since they must necessarily be applied with reference to the state of facts as they exist.

My Government desire further to point out that any replacement which has occurred in the personnel of the administration of Manchuria has been the necessary act of the local population. Even in cases of hostile occupation—which this was not—it is customary for the local officials to remain in the exercise of their functions. In the present case they for the most part fled or resigned; it was their own behaviour which was calculated to destroy the working of the apparatus of government. The Japanese Government cannot think that the Chinese people, unlike all others, are destitute of the power of self-determination and of organizing themselves in order to secure civilized conditions when deserted by the existing officials.

While it need not be repeated that Japan entertains in Manchuria no territorial aims or ambitions, yet, as Your Excellency knows, the welfare and safety of Manchuria and its accessibility for general trade are matters of the deepest interest and of quite extraordinary importance to the Japanese people. That the American Government are always alive to the exigencies of Far Eastern questions has already been made evident on more than one occasion. At the present juncture, when the very existence of our national policy is involved, it is agreeable to be assured that the American Government are devoting in a friendly spirit such sedulous care to the correct appreciation of the situation. . . .

Stimson Summarizes the U. S. Position

To Senator William E. Borah[7]

Washington, February 23, 1932

You have asked my opinion whether, as has been sometimes recently suggested, present conditions in China have in any way indicated that the so-called Nine Power Treaty has become inapplicable or ineffective or rightly in need of modifications, and if so, what I considered should be the policy of this Government.

This Treaty, as you of course know, forms the legal basis upon which now rests the "Open Door" policy towards China. That policy enunciated by John Hay in 1899, brought to an end the struggle among various powers for so-called spheres of interest in China which was threatening the dismemberment of that empire. To accomplish this Mr. Hay invoked two principles (1) equality of commercial opportunity among all nations in dealing with China, and (2) as necessary to that equality the preservation of China's territorial and administrative integrity. These principles were not new in the foreign policy of America. They had been the principles upon which it rested in its dealing with other nations for many years. In the case of China they were invoked to save a situation which not only threatened the future development and sovereignty of that great Asiatic people, but also threatened to create dangerous and constantly increasing rivalries between the other nations of the world. War had already taken place between Japan and China. At the close of that war three other nations intervened to prevent Japan from obtaining some of the results of that war claimed by her. Other nations sought and had obtained spheres of interest. Partly as a result of these actions a serious uprising had broken out in China which endangered the legations of all of the powers at Peking. While the attack on those legations was in progress, Mr. Hay made an announcement in respect to this policy and the principle upon which the powers should act in the settlement of the rebellion. He said:

> The policy of the Government of the United States is to seek a solution which may bring about permanent safety and peace to China, preserve Chinese territorial and administrative entity, protect all rights guaranteed to friendly powers by treaty and international law, and safeguard for the world the principle of equal and impartial trade with all parts of the Chinese Empire.

He was successful in obtaining the assent of the other powers to the policy thus announced.

In taking these steps Mr. Hay acted with the cordial support of the British Government. In responding to Mr. Hay's announcement, above set forth, Lord Salisbury, the British Prime Minister expressed himself "most emphatically as concurring in the policy of the United States."

For twenty years thereafter the Open Door policy rested upon the informal commitments thus made by the various powers. But in the winter of 1921 to 1922, at a conference participated in by all of the principal powers which had interests in the Pacific, the policy was crystallized into the so-called Nine Power Treaty, which gave definition and precision to the principles upon which the policy rested. . . .

This Treaty thus represents a carefully developed and matured international policy intended, on the one hand, to assure to all of the contracting parties their rights and interests in and with regard to China, and on the other hand, to assure to the people of China the fullest opportunity to develop without molestation their sovereignty and independence according to the modern and enlightened standards believed to maintain among the peoples of the earth. At the time this Treaty was signed, it was known that China was engaged in an attempt to develop the free institutions of a self-governing republic after her recent revolution from an autocratic form of government; that she would require many years of both economic and political effort to that end; and that her progress would necessarily be slow. The Treaty was thus a covenant of self-denial among the signatory powers in deliberate renunciation of any policy of aggression which might tend to interfere with that development. It was believed—and the whole history of the development of the "Open Door" policy reveals that faith— that only by such a process, under the protection of such an agreement, could the fullest interests not only of China but of all nations which have intercourse with her best be served.

In its report to the President announcing this Treaty, the American Delegation, headed by the then Secretary of State, Mr. Charles E. Hughes, said:

It is believed that through this Treaty the "Open Door" in China has at last been made a fact.

During the course of the discussions which resulted in the Treaty, the Chairman of the British delegation, Lord Balfour, had stated that:

The British Empire delegation understood that there was no representative of any power around the table who thought that the old practice of "spheres of interest" was either advocated by any government or would be tolerable to this conference. So far as the British Government was concerned, they had, in the most formal manner, publicly announced that they regarded this practice as utterly inappropriate to the existing situation.

At the same time the representative of Japan, Baron Shidehara, announced the position of his government as follows:

No one denies to China her sacred right to govern herself. No one stands in the way of China to work out her own great national destiny.

The Treaty was originally executed by the United States, Belgium, the British Empire, China, France, Italy, Japan, the Netherlands and Portugal. Subsequently it was also executed by Norway, Bolivia, Sweden, Denmark and Mexico. Germany has signed it but her Parliament has not yet ratified it.

It must be remembered also that this Treaty was one of several treaties and agreements entered into at the Washington Conference by the various powers concerned, all of which were interrelated and interdependent. No one of these treaties can be disregarded without disturbing the general understanding and equilibrium which were intended to be accomplished and effected by the group of agreements arrived at in their entirety. The Washington Conference was essentially a disarmament conference, aimed to promote the possibility of peace in the world not only through the cessation of competition in naval armament but also by the solution of various other disturbing problems which threatened the peace of the world, particularly in the Far East. These problems were all interrelated. The willingness of the American government to surrender its then commanding lead in battleship construction and to leave its positions at Guam and in the Philippines without further fortification, was predicated upon, among other things, the self-denying covenants contained in the Nine Power Treaty, which assured the nations of the world not only of equal opportunity for their Eastern trade but also against the military aggrandizement of any other power at the expense of China. One cannot discuss the possibility of modifying or abrogating those provisions of the Nine Power Treaty without considering at the same time the other promises upon which they were really dependent.

Six years later the policy of self-denial against aggression by a stronger against a weaker power, upon which the Nine Power Treaty had been based, received a powerful reinforcement by the execution by substantially all the nations of the world of the Pact of Paris, the so-called Kellogg-Briand Pact. These two treaties represent independent but harmonious steps taken for the purpose of aligning the conscience and public opinion of the world in favor of a system of orderly development by the law of nations including the settlement of all controversies by methods of justice and peace instead of by arbitrary force. The program for the protection of China from outside aggression is an essential part of any such development. The signatories and adherents of the Nine Power Treaty rightly felt that the orderly and peaceful welfare of the 400,000,000 people inhabiting China was necessary to the peaceful welfare of the entire world and that no program for the welfare of the world as a whole could afford to neglect the welfare and protection of China.

The recent events which have taken place in China, especially the hostilities which having been begun in Manchuria have latterly been extended to Shanghai, far from indicating the advisability of any modification of the treaties we have been discussing, have tended to bring home the vital importance of the faithful observance of the covenants therein to all of the nations interested in the Far East. It is not necessary in that connection to inquire into the causes of the controversy or attempt to apportion the blame between the two nations which are unhappily involved; for regardless of cause or responsibility, it is clear beyond peradventure that a situation has developed which cannot, under any circumstances, be reconciled with the obligations of the covenants of these two treaties, and that if the treaties had been faithfully observed such a situation could not have arisen. The signatories of the Nine Power Treaty and of the Kellogg-Briand Pact who are not parties to that conflict are not likely to see any reason for modifying the terms of those treaties. To them the real value of the faithful performance of the treaties has been brought sharply home by the perils and losses to which their nationals have been subjected in Shanghai.

That is the view of this Government. We see no reason for abandoning the enlightened principles which are embodied in these treaties. We believe that this situation would have been avoided had these covenants been faithfully observed, and no evidence has come to us to indicate that a due compliance with them would have interfered with the adequate protection of the legitimate rights in China of the signatories of those treaties and their nationals.

On January 7th last, upon the instruction of the President, this Government formally notified Japan and China that it would not recognize any situation, treaty or agreement entered into by those governments in violation of the covenants of these treaties, which affected the rights of our Government or its citizens in China. If a similar decision should be reached and a similar position taken by the other governments of the world, a caveat will be placed upon such action which, we believe, will effectively bar the legality hereafter of any title or right sought to be obtained by pressure or treaty violation, and which, as has been shown by history in the past, will eventually lead to the restoration to China of rights and titles of which she may have been deprived.

In the past our Government, as one of the leading powers on the Pacific Ocean, has rested its policy upon an abiding faith in the future of the people of China and upon the ultimate success in dealing with them of the principles of fair play, patience, and mutual goodwill. We appreciate the immensity of the task which lies before her statesmen in the development of her country and its government. The delays in her progress, the instability of her attempts to secure a responsible government, were foreseen by Messrs. Hay and Hughes and their contemporaries and were the very obstacles which the policy of the Open Door was designed to meet. We concur with those statesmen, representing all nations in the Washington Conference who decided that China was entitled to the time necessary to accomplish her development. We are prepared to make that our policy for the future. . . .

Henry L. Stimson

Japan Recognizes Manchukuo

That Manchuria had at best been loosely held by the Chinese for some time is reflected in the phrase "China proper," a term often used by scholars and by diplomats on both sides to distinguish Manchuria from the rest of China. Only in the late nineteenth century did Chinese influence begin to be felt in Manchuria, an area that had previously been politically separate and, on more than one occasion, had itself asserted a dominant role over China.

A large movement of ethnic Chinese into Manchuria occurred just prior to the opening of the twentieth century, but Chinese control of Manchuria was limited by increasing Russian and Japanese influence there. While nominally a part of China, Manchuria, like Korea, was destined to become a pawn in the struggle between Russia and Japan, thus affecting the United States as American diplomats tried in vain to preserve the Open Door in all parts of China. The impossibility of doing that was indicated by the various concessions made prior to the 1920s. The Washington treaties had seemingly stabilized the area, though without invalidating previous Japanese and Russian holdings there.

The latent feeling of Manchurian nationalism was utilized by the Japanese as part of their effort to dislodge the region from Chinese suzerainty. With the support of the Japanese military there, an independent Manchuria, renamed Manchukuo (often spelled "Manchoukuo"), was proclaimed in early 1932. In September, Japan extended recognition to the new government. Germany and Italy later granted recognition, but the United States, true to the Stimson Doctrine, refused to even consider recognition during the 1930s. Then, as the Franklin Roosevelt Administration negotiated with Japan in the spring of 1941 in an attempt to avoid war in the Pacific, Manchukuo resurfaced as an important issue in Japanese-American diplomatic relations.

The Japan-"Manchoukuo" Protocol of September 15, 1932[8]

Protocol

Whereas Japan has recognized the fact that Manchoukuo, in accordance with the free will of its inhabitants, has organized and established itself as an independent territory; and

Whereas Manchoukuo has declared its intention of abiding by all international engagements entered into by China in so far as they are applicable to Manchoukuo;

Now the Governments of Japan and Manchoukuo have, for the purpose of establishing a perpetual relationship of good neighborhood between Japan and Manchoukuo, each respecting the territorial rights of the other, and also in order to secure the peace of the Far East, agreed as follows:

1. Manchoukuo shall confirm and respect, in so far as no agreement to the contrary shall be made between Japan and Manchoukuo in the future, all rights and interests possessed by Japan or her subjects within the territory of Manchoukuo by virtue of Sino-Japanese treaties, agreements or other arrangements or Sino-Japanese contracts, private as well as public;

2. Japan and Manchoukuo, recognizing that any threat to the territory or to the peace and order of either of the High Contracting Parties constitutes at the same time a threat to the safety and existence of the other, agree to cooperate in the maintenance of their national security; it being understood that such Japanese forces as may be necessary for this purpose shall be stationed in Manchoukuo. . . .

The present protocol has been drawn up in Japanese and Chinese, two identical copies being made in each language. Should any difference arise in regard to interpretation between the Japanese and the Chinese texts the Japanese text shall prevail. . . .

Chenghsiao-hsu   Nobuyoshi Muto
Prime Minister of Manchoukuo   [Japanese Ambassador]

Japan Withdraws From The League

With neither the League nor the United States willing to use force or an economic embargo to dislodge Japan from Manchuria, opposition to Japanese expansion was confined to verbal condemnation of Japan's action. In a meeting with Ambassador Debuchi early in January 1933, Stimson bluntly suggested that Japan, if unwilling to abide by international agreements, ought to leave the League of Nations. On February 24 that organization formally approved the Lytton (Committee of Nineteen) report, which, though favorable in some respects to Japan, was highly critical of Japanese action in Manchuria. In return, Japan, citing irreconcilable differences with the League, gave the required notification of Japan's intent to withdraw from the organization.

Stimson Suggests Withdrawal

Memorandum by the Secretary of State[9]

Washington, January 5, 1933

The Japanese Ambassador [Katsuji Debuchi] came in with the remark that he regretted that his presence seemed to coincide with a new outbreak of war. He said that . . . from the information he received this affair at Shanghaikwan was a local incident, provoked by a minor outbreak of Chinese against the Japanese there. . . . He said that . . . unless there was further provocation . . . the matter would be controlled. . . . [In] any event Japan had no territorial ambition south of the Great Wall. I reminded the Ambassador that a year ago he had told me Japan had no territorial ambitions in Manchuria. He became flustered and said that that was so but the situation had changed greatly. At any rate, he could now assure me that they had no such ambitions in North China. He said further that in Japan he thought that matters were progressing . . . and he regarded this incident at Shanghaikwan as a test incident as to whether the military elements still remained in control or whether the civil government had regained its position.

I reminded the Ambassador that just before he went away he told me that the Japanese Government was in control of a group of young officers, none of them of a higher rank than a Lieutenant-Colonel, and I said to him that he must recognize that as long as that situation lasted I could not regard Japan as a normal Government and must make my own conclusions as to information coming from her. He said he remembered that situation but he found that when he got back to Japan that it had somewhat changed. . . . But he said he must in all frankness tell me that no Japanese Cabinet which advocated a compromise of the Manchukuo question could survive in Japan; that must be regarded as a closed incident. I told the Ambassador that in that case I could see, on my part, no other course than for Japan to get out of the League of Nations and the Kellogg Pact. I went over the situation of the basic policy of this Government and the rest of the world and Europe, arising out of the Great War which had brought us to the conclusion that another war might destroy our civilization and which had made us determined to support the peace machinery which would render such a recurrence impossible. We recognized that Japan had a right to live her own way, provided she did not break treaties which she had made, and that if she was determined to lead a life differently from what we were determined to do I saw no other way but for her to withdraw from the associations and treaties which we proposed to abide by.

Report of the Committee of Nineteen

Feb. 24, 1933[10]

The Assembly Recommends as Follows:

1. Whereas the sovereignty over Manchuria belongs to China,
   A. Considering that the presence of Japanese troops outside the zone of the South Manchuria Railway and their operations outside this are incompatible with the legal principles which should govern the settlement of the dispute, and that it is necessary to establish as soon as possible a situation consistent with these principles,

The Assembly recommends the evacuation of these troops. In view of the special circumstances of the case, the first object of the negotiations recommended hereinafter should be to organise this evacuation and to determine the methods, stages and time-limits thereof.

B. Having regard to the local conditions special to Manchuria, the particular rights and interests possessed by Japan therein, and the rights and interests of third States,

The Assembly recommends the establishment in Manchuria, within a reasonable period, of an organisation under the sovereignty of, and compatible with the administrative integrity of, China. This organisation should provide a wide measure of autonomy, should be in harmony with local conditions and should take account of the multilateral treaties in force, the particular rights and interests of Japan, the rights and interests of third States, and, in general, the principles and conditions reproduced . . . above; the determination of the respective powers of and relations between the Chinese Central Government and the local authorities should be made the subject of a Declaration by the Chinese Government having the force of an international undertaking. . . .

Section III

In view of the special circumstances of the case, the recommendations made do not provide for a mere return to the *status quo* existing before September, 1931. They likewise exclude the maintenance and recognition of the existing regime in Manchuria, such maintenance and recognition being incompatible with the good understanding between the two countries on which peace in the Far East depends.

It follows that, in adopting the present report, the Members of the League intend to abstain, particularly as regards the existing regime in Manchuria, from any act which might prejudice or delay the carrying out of the recommendations of the said report. They will continue not to recognise this regime either *de jure* or *de facto*. They intend to abstain from taking any isolated action with regard to the situation in Manchuria and to continue to concert their action among themselves as well as with the interested States not members of the League. As regards the Members of the League who are signatories of the Nine Power Treaty, it may be recalled that, in accordance with the provisions of that Treaty: "Whenever a situation arises which, in the opinion of any one of them, involves the application of the stipulations of the present Treaty and renders desirable discussion of such application, there shall be full and frank communication between the contracting Powers concerned."

In order to facilitate as far as possible the establishment in the Far East of a situation in conformity with the recommendations of the present report, the Secretary-General is instructed to communicate a copy of this report to the States non-members of the League who are signatories of, or have acceded to, the Pact of Paris or the Nine Power Treaty, informing them of the Assembly's hope that they will associate themselves with the views expressed in the report, and that they will if necessary, concert their action and their attitude with the Members of the League.

Japan Quits the League

*Telegram From the Minister for Foreign Affairs of Japan
to the Secretary-General*[11]

Tokio, March 27, 1933

The Japanese Government believe that the national policy of Japan, which has for its aim to ensure the peace of the Orient and thereby to contribute to the cause of peace throughout the world, is identical in spirit with the mission of the League of Nations, which is to achieve international peace and security. It has always been with pleasure, therefore, that this country has for thirteen years past, as an original Member of the League and a permanent Member of its Council, extended a full measure of co-operation with her fellow-Members towards the attainment of its high purpose. It is, indeed, a matter of historical fact that Japan has continuously participated in the various activities of the League with a zeal not inferior to that exhibited by any other nation. At the same time, it is and always has been the conviction of the Japanese Government that, in order to render possible the maintenance of peace in various regions of the world, it is necessary in existing circumstances to allow the operation of the Covenant of the League to vary in accordance with the actual conditions prevailing in each of those regions. Only by acting on this just and equitable principle can the League fulfil its mission and increase its influence.

Acting on this conviction, the Japanese Government ever since the Sino-Japanese dispute was, in September 1931, submitted to the League, have, at meetings of the League and on other occasions, continually set forward a consistent view. This was that, if the League was to settle the issue fairly and equitably, and to make a real contribution to the promotion of peace in the Orient, and thus enhance its prestige, it should acquire a complete grasp of the actual conditions in this quarter of the globe and apply the Covenant of the League in accordance with these conditions. They have repeatedly emphasised and insisted upon the absolute necessity of taking into consideration the fact that China is not an organised State; that its internal conditions and external relations are characterised by extreme confusion and complexity and by many abnormal and exceptional features; and that, accordingly, the general principles and usages of international law which govern the ordinary relations between nations are found to be considerably modified in their operation so far as China is concerned, resulting in the quite abnormal and unique international practices which actually prevail in that country.

However, the majority of the Members of the League evinced, in the course of its deliberations during the past seventeen months, a failure either to grasp these realities or else to face them and take them into proper account. Moreover, it has frequently been made manifest in these deliberations that there exist serious differences of opinion between Japan and these Powers concerning the application and even the interpretation of various international engagements and obligations, including the Covenant of the League and the principles of international law. As a result, the report adopted by the Assembly at the special session of February 24th last, entirely misapprehending the spirit of Japan, pervaded as it is by no other desire than the maintenance of peace in the Orient, contains gross errors both in the ascertainment of facts and in the conclusions deduced. In asserting that the action of the Japanese army at the time of the incident of September 18th and subsequently did not fall within the just limits of self-defense, the report assigned no reasons and came to an arbitrary conclusion, and in ignoring alike the state of tension which preceded, and the various aggravations which succeeded, the incident—for all of which the full responsibility is incumbent upon China—the report creates a source of fresh conflict in the political arena of the Orient. By refusing to acknowledge the actual circumstances that led to the foundation of Manchukuo, and by attempting to challenge the position taken up by Japan in recognising the new State, it cuts away the ground for the stabilisation of the Far-Eastern situation. Nor can the terms laid down in its recommendations—as was fully explained in the statement issued by this Government on February 25th last—ever be of any possible service in securing enduring peace in these regions.

The conclusion must be that, in seeking a solution of the question, the majority of the League have attached greater importance to upholding inapplicable formula than to the real task of assuring peace, and higher value to the vindication of academic theses than to the eradication of the sources of future conflict. For these reasons, and because of the profound differences of opinion existing between Japan and the majority of the League in their interpretation of the Covenant and of other treaties, the Japanese Government have been led to realise the existence of an irreconcilable divergence of views, dividing Japan and the League on policies of peace, and especially as regards the fundamental principles to be followed in the establishment of a durable peace in the Far East. The Japanese Government, believing that, in these circumstances, there remains no room for further co-operation, hereby give notice, in accordance with the provisions of Article 1, paragraph 3 of the Covenant, of the intention of Japan to withdraw from the League of Nations.

Notes

1. U. S. Department of State, *Foreign Relations of the United States: Japan: 1931–1941* (Washington, 1943), I, 11–12.
2. *Ibid.*, I, 10.
3. *Ibid.*, I, 27–28
4. *Ibid.*, I, 28–29,
5. *Ibid.*, I, 76.
6. *Ibid.*, I, 76–77.
7. *Ibid.*, I, 83–87.
8. U. S. Department of State, *Foreign Relations of the United States: 1932* (Washington, 1948), IV, 254–255.
9. *Foreign Relations: Japan*, I, 107–108.
10. League of Nations, *Official Journal*, VII, 20–21.
11. *Ibid.*, VII, 657–658.

III

INCREASING TENSION
OVER CHINA

Despite criticism by the League and nonrecognition by the United States, Japan continued to control the client state of Manchukuo. While only Germany and Italy, among the major powers, recognized the new government, the Soviet Union and Britain gave serious consideration to recognition before dropping the idea.

Inauguration of a new American President, Franklin Roosevelt, brought no immediate change in American foreign policy toward Japan. Out-going Secretary of State Stimson, after conferring with the President-elect, had informed Britain that the new administration would follow the nonrecognition policy established by Hoover and Stimson. But that decision must not be seen as a firm endorsement of a hardline, non-appeasement approach to Far Eastern problems. Instead, it reflected the President's desire to concentrate on the depression, which was America's paramount concern, rather than engage in distracting foreign policy matters.

Roosevelt's preoccupation with domestic matters was reflected in a variety of ways that influenced foreign affairs. Recognition of the Soviet Union was predicated in part on the belief that trade with Russia would be facilitated if formal recognition were extended. His scuttling of the London economic conference early in 1933 stemmed from his desire to maintain a free hand in dealing with the domestic economic crisis.

But more directly reflective of the American desire to remain aloof from international concerns that were not in the nation's interest was passage of a series of neutrality acts during Roosevelt's first term. With presidential support and bipartisan agreement, Congress enacted legislation designed to keep the nation out of a second world war should one arise. Restrictions on loans to foreign governments, on use of foreign passenger ships, and on the sale of war material, were all prompted by the belief that these activities had taken the nation into World War I. American isolationists wanted to make certain that similar deeds would not take the United States into World War II.

The depression also had a significant impact upon Japan, where its effect strengthened the anti-western and anti-democratic element in government. Ultranationalists in the military, particularly among the younger army officers, used the economic crisis to gain influence among the people, especially the peasants, suggesting an Asia under Japan's dominance as the solution to the nation's economic problems. Benefiting from a series of assassinations by an ultranationalist faction that silenced opposition from moderate and liberal leaders, expansionists took control of the cabinet in the mid 1930s and pushed ahead with efforts to promote Japan's interests through military action rather than diplomacy.

In July 1937, another incident, this time at the Marco Polo Bridge near Peiping, gave the Japanese an opportunity to seize portions of China proper as they had done in Manchuria in 1931. While skirmishes between armed forces of the two nations had been common for several years, the new action soon became a full scale Japanese invasion of China, justified by the Japanese as necessary to protect their citizens and property there. Although during the Manchurian crisis the League had still represented a potential for peace, little hope was held in 1937 that the organization could halt hostilities. An international conference at Brussels in November failed to find a solution.

The United States feared that much of China was now to go the way of Manchuria and that the Open Door would be permanently closed. Isolationism, still the basic feeling of most Americans, prevented any policy more effective than that followed by the United States in the Manchurian Incident. The Stimson Doctrine of 1932 was matched by President Roosevelt's call for a quarantine in October, 1937. But while the Stimson policy had drawn support both at home and abroad, Roosevelt's plan to quarantine aggressors— he never explained precisely what form the quarantine would take—met with mild response overseas and received severe criticism at home. Some Americans interpreted the sinking of the *Panay* in December to be Japan's reply to the President's speech.

While American interests were directed toward troubles in Europe in 1938, Japanese occupation of Chinese territory continued unabated. The State Department, worried about Japanese intentions, found Japan increasingly reluctant to guarantee the Open Door, at least in the way it had been interpreted by John Hay. There was more frequent talk in Japan about crushing China and about a "New Order" in Asia, a Japanese New Order that seemed incompatible with an American Open Door. When a Japanese-sponsored government for China emerged at Nanking under Wang Ching-wei, who had recently broken with Chiang Kai-shek's Nationalists, the fear of another "Manchukuo" neared realization.

Fighting Resumes in China

For several decades various nations had stationed military forces in China, including the United States, which had naval and marine units there in small numbers. But the Japanese units far exceeded the size of other foreign contingents. Since the Boxer Rebellion a Japanese force had been in North China, assigned the task of maintaining open communication between the coast and Peiping. It was this force that was involved in the clash at the Marco Polo Bridge on July 7, 1937.

The fight that took place between Japanese and Chinese forces at the bridge initially had the appearance of many similar incidents that had involved clashes between Chinese and foreign troops over the years. There was little reason to suspect that this action would escalate into a full scale conflict. The matter-of-fact report sent to Washington the next day by Ambassador Johnson, who was in Peiping, gave no hint that war was near.

The Ambassador in China (Johnson) to the Secretary of State[1]

Peiping, July 8, 1937

A clash took place shortly before midnight last evening at Marco Polo Bridge, which is 10 miles west of Peiping, between Japanese and [Chinese] 29th Army troops. Japanese troops have been maneuvering for some 2 weeks in that vicinity and, according to Chinese sources, attempted last evening to take Marco Polo Bridge as a part of the maneuvers. The Chinese troops which have been stationed at either end of the bridge for a long time resisted and subsequently retired into the nearby small, walled town of Wanpinhsien. It is not known what casualties may have occurred during the clash at the bridge.

. . . Desultory firing was still going on in the vicinity of Marco Polo Bridge as late as 8:30 a.m. today although country this side was peaceful, Chinese on farms going about their affairs as usual. . . .

Johnson

Roosevelt Calls For A Quarantine

While Franklin Roosevelt's first term represented the peak of isolationism in American foreign policy between the two world wars, several factors worked to reverse that policy early in his second term. The landslide victory of 1936 had given him another four years in the White House. Since traditionally presidents did not seek a third term, Roosevelt was now in a position to take action that a first term president might not engage in, unwilling to alienate voters.

Furthermore, in 1933 the likelihood of another world war was remote, but events since then had reached a crisis point. Benito Mussolini had led Italy into Ethiopia; Spain was immersed in a civil war; and Adolf Hitler had made ominous gestures toward Germany's neighbors. The Neutrality Acts had been passed in response to these growing crises.

One other consideration prompted Roosevelt to abandon the isolationism of his first term. He had been elected in 1932 to cope with a great depression. By early 1937 he believed that the economic conditions had so improved that he could now devote more energy to foreign affairs, which he felt were increasingly critical to American interests.

When war broke out in China in 1937, however, the President moved to carry out the spirit of isolationism that Congress had enacted in his first term. When a freighter owned by the American government but leased to a private firm left for China carrying war equipment, he banned the use of government-owned ships for the carrying of munitions to either belligerent and informed private shipping companies that their ships would sail at their own risk. However, the President did not invoke the Neutrality Act, a position that was technically correct since no formal war had been declared.

As the war in China spread in the summer of 1937, Roosevelt turned his attention to the growing threat to peace posed by potential aggressors. By October Japan had taken Peiping, Shanghai was under seige, and the war was rapidly spreading. Anxious to condemn this threat to peace, the President chose a most unusual audience for his announcement. In Chicago, the heartland of American isolationism, at a public ceremony that had nothing to do with foreign policy, the President departed from the isolationism of the early 1930s with a stirring, though undetailed, call for international action.

Chicago, October 5, 1937[2]

. . . It is because the people of the United States under modern conditions must, for the sake of their own future, give thought to the rest of the world, that I, as the responsible executive head of the Nation, have chosen this great inland city and this gala occasion to speak to you on a subject of definite national importance.

The political situation in the world, which of late has been growing progressively worse, is such as to cause grave concern and anxiety to all the peoples and nations who wish to live in peace and amity with their neighbors.

Some 15 [9] years ago the hopes of mankind for a continuing era of international peace were raised to great heights when more than 60 nations solemnly pledged themselves not to resort to arms in furtherance of their national aims and policies. The high aspirations expressed in the Briand-Kellogg Peace Pact and the hopes for peace thus raised have of late given way to a haunting fear of calamity. The present reign of terror and international lawlessness began a few years ago.

It began through unjustified interference in the internal affairs of other nations or the invasion of alien territory in violation of treaties and has now reached a stage where the very foundations of civilization are seriously threatened. The landmarks and traditions which have marked the progress of civilization toward a condition of law, order, and justice are being wiped away.

Without a declaration of war and without warning or justification of any kind, civilians, including women and children, are being ruthlessly murdered with bombs from the air. In times of so-called peace, ships are being attacked and sunk by submarines without cause or notice. Nations are fomenting and taking sides in civil warfare in nations that have never done them any harm. Nations claiming freedom for themselves deny it to others.

Innocent peoples and nations are being cruelly sacrificed to a greed for power and supremacy which is devoid of all sense of justice and humane consideration.

To paraphrase a recent author, "perhaps we foresee a time when men, exultant in the technique of homicide, will rage so hotly over the world that every precious thing will be in danger, every book and picture and harmony, every treasure garnered through two millenniums, the small, the delicate, the defenseless—all will be lost or wrecked or utterly destroyed."

If those things come to pass in other parts of the world let no one imagine that America will escape, that it may expect mercy, that this Western Hemisphere will not be attacked, and that it will continue tranquilly and peacefully to carry on the ethics and the arts of civilization.

If those days come "there will be no safety by arms, no help from authority, no answer in science. The storm will rage till every flower of culture is trampled and all human beings are leveled in a vast chaos."

If those day are not to come to pass—if we are to have a world in which we can breathe freely and live in amity without fear—the peace-loving nations must make a concerted effort to uphold laws and principles on which alone peace can rest secure.

The peace-loving nations must make a concerted effort in opposition to those violations of treaties and those ignorings of humane instincts which today are creating a state of international anarchy and instability from which there is no escape through mere isolation or neutrality.

Those who cherish their freedom and recognize and respect the equal right of their neighbors to be free and live in peace, must work together for the triumph of law and moral principles in order that peace, justice, and confidence may prevail in the world. There must be a return to a belief in the pledged word, in the value of a signed treaty. There must be recognition of the fact that national morality is as vital as private morality. . . .

There is a solidarity and interdependence about the modern world, both technically and morally, which makes it impossible for any nation completely to isolate itself from economic and political upheavals in the rest of the world, especially when such upheavals appear to be spreading and not declining. There can be no stability or peace either within nations or between nations except under laws and moral standards adhered to by all. International anarchy destroys every foundation for peace. It jeopardizes either the immediate or the future security of every nation, large or small. It is therefore, a matter of vital interest and concern to the people of the United States that the sanctity of international treaties and the maintenance of international morality be restored.

The overwhelming majority of the peoples and nations of the world today want to live in peace. They seek the removal of barriers against trade. They want to exert themselves in industry, in agriculture, and in business, that they may increase their wealth through the production of wealth-producing goods rather than striving to produce military planes and bombs and machine guns and cannons for the destruction of human lives and useful property.

In those nations of the world which seem to be piling armament on armament for purposes of aggression, and those other nations which fear acts of aggression against them and their security, a very high proportion of their national income is being spent for armaments. It runs from 30 to as high as 50 percent.

The proportion that we in the United States spend is far less—11 or 12 percent.

How happy we are that the circumstances of the moment permit us to put our money into bridges and boulevards, dams and reforestation, the conservation of our soil, and many other kinds of useful works rather than into huge standing armies and vast supplies of implements of war.

I am compelled and you are compelled, nevertheless, to look ahead. The peace, the freedom, and the security of 90 percent of the population of the world is being jeopardized by the remaining 10 percent who are threatening a breakdown of all international order and law. Surely the 90 percent who want to live in peace under law and in accordance with moral standards that have received almost universal acceptance through the centuries can and must find some way to make their will prevail.

The situation is definitely of universal concern. The questions involved relate not merely to violations of specific provisions of particular treaties; they are questions of war and of peace, of international law, and especially of principles of humanity. It is true that they involve definite violations of agreements, and especially of the Covenant of the League of Nations, the Briand-Kellogg Pact, and the Nine Power Treaty. But they also involve problems of world economy, world security, and world humanity.

It is true that the moral consciousness of the world must recognize the importance of removing injustices and well-founded grievances; but at the same time it must be aroused to the cardinal necessity of honoring sanctity of treaties, of respecting the rights and liberties of others, and of putting an end to acts of international aggression.

It seems to be unfortunately true that the epidemic of world lawlessness is spreading.

When an epidemic of physical disease starts to spread, the community approves and joins in a quarantine of the patients in order to protect the health of the community against the spread of the disease.

It is my determination to pursue a policy of peace and to adopt every practicable measure to avoid involvement in war. It ought to be inconceivable that in this modern era, and in the face of experience, any nation could be so foolish and ruthless as to run the risk of plunging the whole world into war by invading and violating in contravention of solemn treaties the territory of other nations that have done them no real harm and which are too weak to protect themselves adequately. Yet the peace of the world and the welfare and security of every nation is today being threatened by that very thing.

No nation which refuses to exercise forbearance and to respect the freedom and rights of others can long remain strong and retain the confidence and respect of other nations. No nation ever loses its dignity or good standing by conciliating its differences and by exercising great patience with and consideration for the rights of other nations.

War is a contagion, whether it be declared or undeclared. It can engulf states and peoples remote from the original scene of hostilities. We are determined to keep out of war, yet we cannot insure ourselves against the disastrous effects of war and the dangers of involvement. We are adopting such measures as will minimize our risk of involvement, but we cannot have complete protection in a world of disorder in which confidence and security have broken down.

If civilization is to survive the principles of the Prince of Peace must be restored. Shattered trust between nations must be revived.

Most important of all, the will for peace on the part of peace-loving nations must express itself to the end that nations that may be tempted to violate their agreements and the rights of others will desist from such a cause. There must be positive endeavors to preserve peace.

America hates war. America hopes for peace. Therefore, America actively engages in the search for peace.

The Sinking Of The *Panay*

Following Roosevelt's "Quarantine Speech" an international conference met at Brussels in November. Calling together the nine powers that had signed the Washington Treaty in 1922 dealing with China, the conference attempted to seek a solution to the current turmoil. The Japanese refused to attend, insisting that China and Japan should resolve the dispute themselves. After nearly a month the conference adjourned with an appeal for a cease-fire so that outside powers might mediate the dispute.

In the meantime, as the war spread, the United States prepared to evacuate its nationals from China. The total number of Americans in China when war broke out in 1937 was unknown, but the State Department guessed that 10,000 Americans were in the country in late 1936.

For the protection of American nationals, the United States had a small number of military personnel stationed in China. As of early December, there were 1300 American marines and army personnel at Peiping and Tientsin, stationed there pursuant to the Boxer Protocol of 1901, the same agreement that had permitted Japan to keep troops near Peiping. In addition, over 2500 marines were at Shanghai. The American navy, by virtue of an 1858 treaty with China, had naval detachments in Chinese waters. In early December only nine gunboats, with a total personnel of about 1000 men, were in China.

One of those ships, the *Panay*, was on the Yangtze River near Nanking, where it had been placed for removal and protection of Americans evacuating that city. On Dec. 11, as fighting increased near Nanking and shells began falling in the water near the vessel, the *Panay* moved upstream several miles. As the ship, accompanied by several other foreign vessels, coursed upriver, shells from Japanese guns onshore fell ahead and off the port bow. On the 12th, shelling began again in the morning and the *Panay* moved farther upstream, anchoring twenty-seven miles from Nanking. At 1:30 p.m. the Japanese air attack began.

Hull Protests the Sinking of the *Panay*

Secretary of State Cordell Hull to
Japanese Foreign Minister Koki Hirota

Washington, December 13, 1937

The Government and people of the United States have been deeply shocked by the facts of the bombardment and sinking of the U. S. S. *Panay* and the sinking or burning of the American steamers *Meiping, Meian* and *Meisian [Meihsia]* by Japanese aircraft.

The essential facts are that these American vessels were in the Yangtze River by uncontested and incontestable right; that they were flying the American flag; that they were engaged in their legitimate and appropriate business; that they were at the moment conveying American official and private personnel away from points where danger had developed; that they had several times changed their position, moving upriver, in order to avoid danger; and that they were attacked by Japanese bombing planes. With regard to the attack, a responsible Japanese naval officer at Shanghai has informed the Commander-in-Chief of the American Asiatic Fleet that the four vessels were proceeding upriver; that a Japanese plane endeavored to ascertain their nationality, flying at an altitude of three hundred meters, but was unable to distinguish the flags; that three Japanese bombing planes, six Japanese fighting planes, six Japanese bombing places, and two Japanese bombing planes, in sequence, made attacks which resulted in the damaging of one of the American steamers, and the sinking of the U. S. S. *Panay* and the other two steamers.

Since the beginning of the present unfortunate hostilities between Japan and China, the Japanese Government and various Japanese authorities at various points have repeatedly assured the Government and authorities of the United States that it is the intention and purpose of the Japanese government and the Japanese armed forces to respect fully the rights and interests of other powers. On several occasions, however, acts of Japanese armed forces have violated the rights of the United States, have seriously endangered the lives of American nationals, and have destroyed American property. In several instances, the Japanese Government has admitted the facts, has expressed regrets, and has given assurances that every precaution will be taken against recurrence of such incidents. In the present case, acts of Japanese armed forces have taken place in complete disregard of American rights, have taken American life, and have destroyed American property both public and private.

In these circumstances, the Government of the United States requests and expects of the Japanese Government a formally recorded expression of regret, an undertaking to make complete and comprehensive indemnifications, and an assurance that definite and specific steps have been taken which will ensure that hereafter American nationals, interests and property in China will not be subjected to attack by Japanese armed forces or unlawful interference by any Japanese authorities or forces whatsoever.

> Cordell Hull
> Secretary of State

Japan Replies

Foreign Minister Hirota to American Ambassador Joseph C. Grew[4]

Tokyo, December 14, 1937

Monsieur l'Ambassadeur: Regarding the incident of the 12th December in which the United States gunboat *Panay* and three steamers belonging to the Standard Oil Company were sunk by the bombing of the Japanese naval aircraft on the Yangtze River at a point about twenty-six miles above Nanking, I had the honor, as soon as unofficial information of the incident was brought to my knowledge, to request Your Excellency to transmit to the Government of the United States the apologies of the Japanese Government. From the reports subsequently received from our representatives in China, it has been established that the Japanese naval air force, acting upon information that the Chinese troops fleeing from Nanking were going up the river in the steamers, took off to pursue them, and discovered such vessels at the above-mentioned point. Owing to poor visibility, however, the aircraft, although they descended to fairly low altitudes, were unable to discern any mark to show that any one of them was an American ship or man-of-war. Consequently, the United States gunboat *Panay* and the vessels of the Standard Oil company, being taken for Chinese vessels carrying the fleeing Chinese troops, were bombed and sunk.

While it is clear, in the light of the above circumstances, that the present incident was entirely due to a mistake, the Japanese Government regret most profoundly that it has caused damages to the United States man-of-war and ships and casualties among those on board, and desire to present hereby sincere apologies. The Japanese Government will make indemnifications for all the losses and will deal appropriately with those responsible for the incident. Furthermore, they have already issued strict orders to the authorities on the spot with a view to preventing the recurrence of a similar incident.

The Japanese Government, in the fervent hope that the friendly relations between Japan and the United States will not be affected by this unfortunate affair, have frankly stated as above their sincere attitude which I beg Your Excellency to make known to your Government.

Koki Hirota
Japanese Foreign Minister

Japan Apologizes

Hirota to Grew[5]

Tokyo, December 24, 1937

Monsieur l'Ambassadeur: Regarding the unfortunate incident occurring on the Yangtze River . . . I desire to state that while it is concluded in Your Excellency's note that the incident resulted from disregard of American rights by Japanese armed forces, it was entirely due to a mistake, as has been described in my note. . . . As a result of the thorough investigations which have been continued since then in all possible ways to find out the real causes, it has now been fully established that the attack was entirely unintentional. I trust that this has been made quite clear to Your Excellency through the detailed explanations made to Your Excellency on the 23rd instant by our naval and military authorities.

With reference to the first two items of the requests mentioned in Your Excellency's note, namely, a recorded expression of regret, and indemnifications, no word needs to be added to what I have said in my afore-mentioned note. As regards the guarantee for the future, I wish to inform Your Excellency that the Japanese Navy issued without delay strict orders to "exercise the greatest caution in every area where warships and other vessels of America or any other third power are present, in order to avoid a recurrence of a similar mistake, even at the sacrifice of a strategic advantage in attacking the Chinese troops." Furthermore, rigid orders have been issued to the military, naval, and Foreign Office authorities to pay, in the light of the present untoward incident, greater attention than hitherto to observance of the instructions that have been repeatedly given against infringement of, or unwarranted interference with, the rights and interests of the United States and other third powers. And the Japanese Government are studying carefully every possible means of achieving more effectively the above-stated aims, while they have already taken steps to ascertain, in still closer contact with American authorities in China, the whereabouts of American interests and nationals, and to improve the means of communicating intelligence thereof speedily and effectively to the authorities on the spot.

Although the attack on the man-of-war and other vessels of the United States was due to a mistake . . . the commander of the flying force concerned was immediately removed from his post, and recalled, on the grounds of a failure to take the fullest measures of precaution. Moreover, the staff members of the fleet and the commander of the flying squadron and all others responsible have been duly dealt with according to law. The Japanese Government are thus endeavoring to preclude absolutely all possibility of the recurrence of incidents of a similar character. It needs hardly be emphasized that, of all the above-mentioned measures taken by the Japanese Government, the recall of the commander of the flying force has a significance of special importance. It is my fervent hope that the fact will be fully appreciated by the Government of the United States that this drastic step has been taken solely because of the sincere desire of the Japanese Government to safeguard the rights and interests of the United States and other third powers.

Koki Hirota

Hull Accepts

Hull to Hirota[6]

Washington, December 25, 1937

The Government of the United States refers to its note of December 14 [13], the Japanese Government's note of December 14 and the Japanese Government's note of December 24 in regard to the attack by Japanese armed forces upon the U. S. S. *Panay* and three American merchant ships. . . .

The Government of the United States observed with satisfaction the promptness with which the Japanese Government in its note of December 14 admitted responsibility, expressed regret, and offered amends.

The Government of the United States regards the Japanese Government's account, as set forth in the ... note of December 24, of action taken by it as responsive to the request made by the Government of the United States. ...

With regard to the facts of the origins, causes and circumstances of the incident, ... the Government of the United States relies on the report of findings of the Court of Inquiry of the United States Navy, a copy of which has been communicated officially to the Japanese Government.

It is the earnest hope of the ... United States that the steps which the Japanese Government has taken will prove effective toward preventing any further attacks upon or unlawful interference by Japanese authorities or forces with American nationals, interests or property in China.

Hull

Hirota's Christmas Present

The Ambassador in Japan (Grew) to the Secretary of State[7]

Tokyo, December 26, 1937

... Note delivered to the Minister for Foreign Affairs at noon today.

After I had read the note aloud, Hirota said to me: "I heartily thank your Government and you yourself for this decision. I am very, very happy. You have brought me a splendid Christmas present." The Minister added that the Japanese Government has taken and will continue to take all possible measures to prevent the recurrence of such an incident.

Joseph C. Grew

Japan's "New Order" In Asia

"New Orders" were on the minds of several powers in the 1930s. In Europe, Germany and Italy looked forward to a New Order there that would place those two nations in positions of influence commensurate with their rightful place in the European community. In Asia, Japan would speak of a New Order that envisioned Japan as the focal point of Asiatic development.

With a burgeoning population, relatively little arable land, and a noticeable shortage of those raw materials needed by an industrializing nation, it is not surprising that Japan looked upon East Asia as the solution to the country's economic and social problems. But much of the valuable resources of that part of Asia were already held by western powers, and those sections that remained independent were often subject to the influence of the west. Japan's task, as stated by more militant nationalists in the 1930s, was to liberate the oppressed people of Asia from a debilitating western influence and to substitute for it Japanese domination of the Far East.

The concept of a Japanese "Monroe Doctrine" in Asia was not new in the 1930s. The Japanese had for years argued that geographical proximity to East Asia had given that nation a special interest in that region, entitling Japan to economic and political rights that non-Asian nations could not claim. The genealogy of that policy is found in Taft-Katsura, Root-Takahira, and Lansing-Ishii.

Following Japan's conquest of Manchuria this idea began to crystallize into a more formal policy. In 1934 the foreign office announced a plan designed to discourage Chinese economic cooperation with powers other than Japan. Ignored by both China and the western nations, the announcement nevertheless was indicative of the policy Japan would follow in the years prior to the outbreak of war with the United States in 1941.

The Greater East Asia Co-Prosperity Sphere, as it would later be titled, included Japanese economic hegemony over Korea, Manchukuo, China, the Philippines, Indochina, British Malaya, and the Dutch East Indies. At one point Foreign Minister Koki Hirota had unsuccessfully suggested a bilateral agreement whereby the United States would be dominant in the Eastern Pacific while recognizing the Western Pacific as a Japanese sphere.

The United States viewed such proposals as violations of the Open Door and of the Washington System, whereby developments in the Pacific and the Far East were to be under international, not bilateral, control. Japan could see no difference between a Monroe Doctrine that placed the western hemisphere under American control and a New Order that placed Asia under Japanese control. American diplomats, on the other hand, drew a sharp distinction between the two policies and, especially in 1941, would attempt to distinguish between a policy based on mutual cooperation and respect (the Monroe Doctrine) and one based on conquest and domination (Japan's New Order.)

While the west would not accept Japan's New Order for Asia, the Japanese proceeded with it. In 1940 it was written into a formal treaty, signed by Japan, Manchukuo, and the pro-Japanese government of Wang Ching-wei, the government for occupied China at Nanking.

The "New Order in East Asia" Summarized

Statement by the Japanese Government[8]

November 3, 1938

By the august virtue of His Majesty, our naval and military forces have captured Canton and the three cities of Wuhan; and all the vital areas of China have thus fallen into our hands. The Kuomintang Government exists no longer except as a mere local regime. However, so long as it persists in its anti-Japanese and pro-communist policy our country will not lay down its arms—never until that regime is crushed.

What Japan seeks is the establishment of a new order which will insure the permanent stability of East Asia. In this lies the ultimate purpose of our present military campaign.

This new order has for its foundation a tripartite relationship of mutual aid and co-ordination between Japan, Manchoukuo and China in political, economic, cultural and other fields. Its object is to secure international justice, to perfect the joint defence against Communism, and to create a new culture and realize a close economic cohesion throughout East Asia. This indeed is the way to contribute toward the stabilization of East Asia and the progress of the world.

What Japan desires of China is that that country will share in the task of bringing about this new order in East Asia. She confidently expects that the people of China will fully comprehend her true intentions and that they will respond to the call of Japan for co-operation. Even the participation of the Kuomintang Government would not be rejected, if, repudiating the policy which has guided it in the past and remolding its personnel, so as to translate its re-birth into fact, it were to come forward to join in the establishment of the new order.

Japan is confident that other Powers will on their part correctly appreciate her aims and policy and adapt their attitude to the new conditions prevailing in East Asia. For the cordiality hitherto manifested by the nations which are in sympathy with us, Japan wishes to express her profound gratitude.

The establishment of a new order in East Asia is in complete conformity with the very spirit in which the Empire was founded; to achieve such a task is the exalted responsibility with which our present generation is entrusted. It is, therefore, imperative to carry out all necessary internal reforms, and with a full development of the aggregate national strength, material as well as moral, fulfil at all costs this duty incumbent upon our nation.

Such the Government declare to be the immutable policy and determination of Japan.

Open Door and New Order in Conflict

Foreign Minister Hachiro Arita to Ambassador Grew[9]

Tokyo, November 18, 1938

... While the Japanese Government with the intention of fully respecting American rights and interests in China, as has been frequently stated above, has been making every effort in that direction in view of the fact that military operations on a scale unprecedented in our history are now being carried out in East Asia, I am of the opinion that the Government of Your Excellency's country also should recognize the fact that occasionally obstacles arise hindering the effecting of the intention of respecting the rights and interests of Your Excellency's country.

At present Japan, devoting its entire energy to the establishment of a new order based on genuine international justice throughout East Asia, is making rapid strides toward the attainment of this objective. The successful accomplishment of this purpose is not only indispensible to the existence of Japan, but also constitutes the very foundation of the enduring peace and stability of East Asia.

It is the firm conviction of the Japanese Government that now, at a time of the continuing development of new conditions in East Asia, an attempt to apply to present and future conditions without any changes concepts and principles which were applicable to conditions prevailing before the present incident does not in any way contribute to the solution of immediate issues and further does not in the least promote the firm establishment of enduring peace in East Asia.

The Imperial Government, however, does not have any intention of objecting to the participation in the great work of the reconstruction of East Asia by Your Excellency's country or by other Powers in all fields of trade and industry, when such participation is undertaken with an understanding of the purport of the above stated remarks; and further, I believe that the regimes now being formed in China are also prepared to welcome such participation.

Hachiro Arita

Embassy Counselor Eugene Dooman Recalls a Conversation[10]

Tokyo, November 19, 1938

... After an exchange of amenities, Mr. Arita asked me at the outset how the Ambassador had reacted to the note [printed above] which was handed to me last evening at the Foreign Office. I replied that the Ambassador had examined the note with the best of good will but that he was unable to find in it any statement which was substantially responsive to the desires of the American Government. Mr. Arita said "Well I suppose not."

Mr. Arita remarked that we were meeting, of course, informally and as old friends, and that he felt that he could express himself freely to me not only because he could use the medium of his own language, but he need not be unduly reserved.

There were two important features which inhered in the present position of Japan which, Mr. Arita thought, it was extremely important that the United States and other interested countries should understand. He wondered whether the principle of the open door and equality of opportunity was being applied by international agreement in any part of the world other than China. I here interjected the remark that it was, but Mr. Arita asked me to allow him an opportunity to express his thoughts uninterruptedly. He admitted that here and there, notably in the Congo Basin, the principle of the open door had been established by international agreement, but China, by reasons of its political status, its territorial extent, and its population, was an exception. He then went into an extended account of the origin and development of the application of the principle of the open door to China. He dwelt on the fact that toward the end of the last century the tendency was becoming more clearly defined for certain of the European powers to establish spheres of influence in China and otherwise to endeavor to set up privileged economic and perhaps political positions in China; and he referred to the fact that Japan at that time was a weak country and was incapable of itself setting up any sphere of influence in China, and that Japan had associated itself with the United States in efforts to have that principle accepted as a rule of conduct in China. He, however, emphasized that the principle of the open door was at first applied only to matters of relatively small importance, such as equality of treatment with regard to transportation, customs duties, and so on. It became apparent after the Washington treaty was concluded that the motive of most of the powers in supporting the principle of the open door was to exploit China largely as they had been exploiting Africa.

He then proceeded to his next point. The United States and the British Empire, he said, were important and large territorial, political, and economic entities. They possessed great wealth, they were rich in all the important primary commodities, and there existed in each a rich domestic market. They were, for all practical purposes, largely self-contained, to say nothing of having the resources of wealth and manpower necessary to maintain effective systems of national defense. They could look with almost complete indifference on any attempt on the part of other powers to impose on them economic sanctions. Japan was, however, in an entirely different position. Although Japan had a fairly large population, its area is limited and it possesses few resources. The League of Nations some time ago, invoking Article 16 of the Covenant, had attempted to impose economic sanctions on Italy, which attempt was not successful, and it was his opinion that Japan need no longer be apprehensive of similar action being undertaken by the League against Japan. There were, however, outside of the League of Nations as well as within, several powerful nations whose peoples were predisposed to discuss the possibility of economic sanctions being imposed on Japan. Fortunately, no definite project along those lines has so far been formally brought forward, but the possibility that some serious and concerted effort along these lines might be made was a matter of concern to Japan. Mr. Arita went on to say that there are two ways by which one nation or a group of nations might force another nation to its knees. The first method was obviously the military, by which he meant warships, soldiers, munitions, and so on. The great powers were all supplied with military and naval establishments, and even the smaller nations were equipped with armies and navies consonant with their financial resources. Japan, like other nations, was maintaining military and naval forces adequate for national defense needs. However, there was another method by which pressure could be exerted on Japan, and that was by withholding from her foreign markets and raw materials necessary for her existence. Her army and navy would be useless against pressure applied in that form. It had, therefore, become necessary for Japan to place herself in a position to resist that method of applying pressure, and she was now in process of putting herself in that position by acquiring certain access to necessary raw materials.

The word "bloc" was being frequently used in connection with the economic cooperation between Japan, China, and "Manchukuo", which is now under contemplation. He himself deplored the use of the word "bloc" as it was one which was capable of causing serious misunderstanding; and if he used the word in his conversation with me he did so only for the purposes of convenience and to describe a certain economic and commercial interrelation which would be evolved between the three countries. What is contemplated is to provide Japan with a market analogous to that which the United States and the British Empire each has internal to itself—a market which is one of the important factors in making that nation safe against pressure applied by other nations in the form of sanctions. He emphasized again that the economic linking together of the three countries would not be in any way comparable to the political linking up of the various elements within the British Empire. He could say definitely that Japan has no intention whatever of assimilating politically any part of China or of "Manchukuo", and he saw no inconsistency between the statement and the settled policy of economically linking together the three countries in order to provide for their common security. Such an arrangement would not necessarily be exclusive of American and other foreign enterprise and capital. What the Japanese Government has in mind is that the new bloc, while providing Japan a market and a source for raw materials, will offer other countries an opportunity for trade and for investments, just as the various parts of the United States or of the British Empire, while offering a large domestic market, trade with other parts of the world and offer opportunities for investment of foreign capital.

Mr. Arita went on to say that there prevails a widespread feeling that the Japanese Government has now adopted a new policy—one of closing the open door in China. There had, in fact, been no change in policy. His several predecessors had on several occasions given assurances to the American, British, and other representatives in Tokyo that Japan would respect the principle of the open door. As a matter of fact, those assurance were not intended to be unconditional, for the reason that the time had passed when Japan could give an unqualified undertaking to respect the open door in China. He was not implying that his predecessors had given the assurances in bad faith; on the contrary, he felt certain that they were acting in the best of faith, but what they were attempting to do was to reconcile the principle of the open door with Japan's actual needs and objectives, and that could not be done. As he had previously explained, those objectives are to provide Japan with a market secure against any possible threat of economic sanctions and to acquire safe sources of necessary raw materials; but within those limits Japan was prepared to guarantee equality of opportunity. There would be given full consideration to those enterprises conducted by foreigners other than Japanese which would in no way conflict with or obstruct the carrying out of these primary objectives, and with respect to those enterprises, whether industrial, commercial, or financial, the Japanese Government was fully prepared to give unqualified guarantees. But with regard to other undertakings which overlapped the Japanese economic defense plans, it was no longer possible for Japan to extend any such guarantees. When he came into office, he decided that it would be mischievous as well as useless to attempt to reconcile the principle of the open door, as understood in the United States and elsewhere abroad, with the new situation which Japan was endeavoring to bring about. He therefore declined to repeat those assurances in the note which was yesterday sent to the American Government.

From that point Mr. Arita passed on to the Japanese note. Our note of October 6 had definitely raised the principle of the open door and equality of opportunity, and our Government would no doubt be surprised that the Japanese note did not address itself at length and more definitely to the issues raised by the American Government. The only position which he could have taken in any official note intended for publication would, in the light of the present state of public opinion in Japan, merely have opened up a dispute over principles which he was most anxious to avoid. There were, on the other hand, a number of things he would like to have said in the note but which he could not. It was for these reasons that he looked forward to an opportunity to communicating privately to the Ambassador certain views which would enable the American Government to understand Japan's position.

He realized that there were extended historical and even sentimental associations in the United States with regard to that principle, for the establishment of which Mr. Hay deserved great credit; but it was his feeling that if the Japanese Government had entered into a discussion on the question of principle the possibility of making progress towards some final understanding would have to be abandoned. It was his sincere belief that, with the conversation which he would have on Monday with Mr. Grew, which he hoped would be followed by many others, it would be possible for the two Governments to acquaint each with the problems of the other and thus open the road for a solution on some practical basis by arriving at a new definition of the open door which would be mutually acceptable. He said that on the previous occasion when he was Minister for Foreign Affairs, which was about two years ago, the relations between the United States and Japan had on the whole been satisfactory, and he had taken occasion in his annual address to the Diet to express appreciation of the attitude of fairness which was being shown by the American people toward Japan. Since the outbreak of the present conflict with China, the Japanese people had consistently been appreciative of the openminded attitude of the American Government, and, although he was sorry to say that anger against and disapproval of Japan were universal in the United States, nevertheless the Japanese people still entertained good will toward the United States; but he was confident that by quiet discussion between the two governments and by refraining from engaging in disputes through exchanges of official notes which are later made public, substantial progress could be made toward an eventual satisfactory solution of the present difficulty.

The foregoing is a summary of the statements which Mr. Arita made without interruption over a period of about one hour. When he concluded, I said that there was very little I could say to him either officially or unofficially. There was one thing I could say which it might perhaps be difficult for the Ambassador to say to him at their forthcoming interview, and it was this: This American Government has been showing, as Mr. Arita would readily recognize, extraordinary restraint in the face of the constant and widespread violations of the rights of American citizens in China. It was a striking commentary on that restraint when the American Government waited fifteen months to bring the question of the principle of the open door to a head. During that time, the instances of wilful and sinister attempts to injure American interests were innumerable—I thought they might well amount into the hundreds. Some of these cases had occurred, it is true, as a result of Japanese military operations, but I felt on safe ground in saying that the majority of these cases might well have been avoided if the Japanese military commanders in China and their civilian advisers, among the latter of which there appeared to be a large proportion of unscrupulous persons, had even an elementary sense of respect for the rights of others.

Mr. Arita said that he did not wish to be understood as contradicting my statement that cases of the sort I described had occurred, but he wondered whether we had taken into full account the conditions which attend large scale military operations. I replied that I had taken that fact into full account, and I recited several cases of interference with American rights which had recently occurred in Shanghai, which I pointed out was now several hundred miles away from any important theatre of hostilities.

After some further discussion on the point mentioned in the previous paragraph, Mr. Arita said that he was looking forward very keenly to his conversation with Mr. Grew on Monday, and that he hoped that I would report to Mr. Grew all that he (Mr. Arita) had said to me. He thought it unlikely that he would go over all the same ground again with Mr. Grew but he thought it would be useful to Mr. Grew to know the fundamental position of the Japanese Government.

I expressed to Mr. Arita my thanks for his courtesy in receiving me, and I said that I would go at once to see Mr. Grew and report the terms of the conversation.

Eugene H. Dooman

The United States Rejects the New Order

The American Ambassador in Japan (Grew) to the
Japanese Minister for Foreign Affairs (Arita)[11]

Tokyo, December 30, 1938

Excellency: Acting under the instructions of my Government I have the honor to address to Your Excellency the following note:

The Government of the United States has received and has given full consideration to the [note] of the Japanese Government of November 18. . . .

The Government of the United States expresses its conviction that the restrictions and measures under reference not only are unjust and unwarranted but are counter to the provisions of several binding international agreements, voluntarily entered into, to which both Japan and the United States, and in some cases other countries, are parties. . . .

The Government of the United States in its note of October 6 requested, in view of the oft reiterated assurances proffered by the Government of Japan of its intention to observe the principles of equality of opportunity in its relations with China and in view of Japan's treaty obligations so to do, that the Government of Japan abide by these obligations and carry out these assurances in practice. The Japanese Government in its reply appears to affirm that it is its intention to make its observance of that principle conditional upon an understanding by the American

Government and by other governments of a "new situation" and a "new order" in the Far East as envisaged and fostered by Japanese authorities. . . .

Fundamental principles such as the principle of equality of opportunity which have long been regarded as inherently wise and just, which have been widely adopted and adhered to, and which are general in their application are not subject to nullification by a unilateral affirmation. . . .

In the light of these facts, and with reference especially to the purpose and the character of the treaty provisions from time to time solemnly agreed upon for the very definite purposes indicated, the Government of the United States deprecates the fact that one of the parties to these agreements has chosen to embark—as indicated both by action of its agents and by official statements of its authorities—upon a course directed toward the arbitrary creation by that power by methods of its own selection, regardless of treaty pledges and the established rights of other powers concerned, of a "new order" in the Far East. Whatever may be the changes which have taken place in the situation in the Far East and whatever may be the situation now, these matters are of no less interest and concern to the American Government than have been the situations which have prevailed there in the past, and such changes as may henceforth take place there, changes which may enter into the producing of a "new situation" and a "new order," are and will be of like concern to this Government. This Government is well aware that the situation has changed. This Government is also well aware that many of the changes have been brought about by the action of Japan. This Government does not admit, however, that there is need or warrant for any one Power to take upon itself to prescribe what shall be the terms and conditions of a "new order" in areas not under its sovereignty and to constitute itself the repository of authority and the agent of destiny in regard thereto. . . .

The Government of the United States has at all times regarded agreements as susceptible of alteration, but it has always insisted that alterations can rightfully be made only by orderly processes of negotiation and agreement among the parties thereto.

The Japanese Government has upon numerous occasions expressed itself as holding similar views. . . .

Meanwhile, this Government reserves all rights of the United States as they exist and does not give assent to any impairment of any of those rights.

Joseph C. Grew

The New Order Takes Shape

Joint Declaration by the Governments of Japan, "Manchukuo,"
and the Wang Ching-wei Regime in Japanese-occupied China[12]

Signed at Nanking, November 30, 1940

The Imperial Government of Japan;
The Imperial Government of Manchoukuo; and
The National Government of the Republic of China:

Being desirous that the three countries respect one another's inherent characteristics and closely cooperate with one another as good neighbours under their common ideal of establishing a new order in East Asia on an ethical basis, constituting thereby the mainstay of a permanent peace in East Asia, and with this as a nucleus contributing toward the peace of the world in general, declare as follows:

1. Japan, Manchoukuo and China will respect mutually their sovereignty and territories.
2. Japan, Manchoukuo and China will bring about general co-operation on a reciprocal basis among the three countries, especially a good neighbourly friendship, common defense against communistic activities and economic co-operation, and for that purpose will take all the necessary measures in every direction.
3. Japan, Manchoukuo and China will promptly conclude agreements in accordance with the present Declaration. . . .

Notes

1. *Foreign Relations: Japan*, I, 313.
2. *Ibid.*, I, 379–383
3. *Ibid.*, I, 523–524.
4. *Ibid.*, I, 525.
5. *Ibid.*, I, 549–550
6. *Ibid.*, I, 551–552.
7. *Ibid.*, I, 552.
8. *Ibid.*, I, 477–478.
9. *Ibid.*, I, 797–800.
10. *Ibid.*, I, 801–806.
11. *Ibid.*, I, 820–826.
12. *Ibid.*, II, 128.

IV

JAPANESE EXPANSION IN A WORLD CONTEXT

When fighting renewed in Asia in 1937 it could no longer be looked upon as a Far Eastern problem, unrelated to developments elsewhere. The pattern for expansion that the Japanese had used in 1931 was repeated in Europe and Africa where the fascist nations, Germany and Italy, exhibited aggressive tendencies. Observers of world affairs noted a striking similarity in the expansionist policies of Germany, Italy, and Japan. The joining of these three nations in an anti-communist pact was evidence of a close relationship between developments in the Far East and Europe.

A further indication of the tie between events in Asia and in Europe was seen in the changing trade relations between the United States and Japan after war broke out in Europe in September 1939. In the summer of 1940 the United States, which earlier in the year had formally ended its 1911 commercial treaty with Japan, began to apply economic pressure on the Japanese through the imposition of an ever lengthening list of items that could not be exported to Japan. While technically no nation was singled out in the Presidential decree banning such exports, the net effect of the non-exportation program was more harmful to Japan than to any other country.

With the occupation by Japan of northern French Indochina in late summer, American statesmen began to reshape their Asian policy in the light of European developments. The outbreak of war in Europe had complicated what had heretofore been strictly an Asian matter. Without altering American opposition to Japanese imperialism diplomats now found it necessary to view Japanese moves as but one part of a larger diplomatic puzzle in which European events were considered paramount. American actions and reactions in the Pacific were to be taken only after considering the effect such moves would have on Europe. To December 7, 1941, and indeed throughout World War II, the United States continued to consider Japanese expansion as extremely serious but secondary to American interests in Europe.

When Japan joined with Germany and Italy to create the Tripartite, or Axis, Alliance later in 1940, the United States feared that peace in the Pacific had become directly dependent upon continued United States neutrality in the European War. But Japan still faced two major powers in the Far East, Russia and the United States, a fact that might have kept Japan in check. In April 1941, however, the Soviet Union was neutralized by a nonaggression pact with Japan, and the United States stood almost alone.

The Anti-Comintern Pact

In the lull between the truce in Manchuria and the outbreak of war in 1937 Japan faced isolation as other powers, fearful of losing more of China to Japanese expansion, rallied to the aid of China. Britain, Germany, and the United States extended various forms of aid.

Within China, Chiang Kai-shek's Nationalists were stabilizing their control. They had carried out successful monetary reforms, were aggressive in efforts to rebuild the economy and, with German support, had made strides toward strengthening their military. Chinese communists, who had been at odds with the Japanese since the occupation of Manchuria, sought to renew the conflict with Japan, fearing that Japan would extend its control into other parts of China currently held by the communists.

In 1935 the Russians had embarked on a policy of cooperation with other governments against fascists in Europe and Asia. Japan interpreted this as a threat to her holdings on the mainland. While momentarily China was divided between the communists and Chiang's Nationalists, should they unite, as they did temporarily at the end of 1936, Japanese expansion on the mainland would be seriously hampered.

Fearful of Russian resurgence in the Far East, a resurgence made doubly dangerous by the fact that it would now be led by a communist Russia, Japan looked toward Germany, whose location just beyond Russia's western frontier made Germany an especially valuable ally. In November 1936, shortly after Hitler and Mussolini had agreed to a policy of cooperation, Japan and Germany signed an anti-communist alliance. In 1937 Italy joined the pact.

Agreement between Japan and Germany

Agreement Guarding Against the Communistic International[1]

Berlin, November 25, 1936

The Imperial Government of Japan and the Government of Germany,

In cognizance of the fact that the object of the Communistic International (the so-called Komintern) is the disintegration of, and the commission of violence against, existing States by the exercise of all means at its command,

Believing that the toleration of interference by the Communistic International in the internal affairs of nations not only endangers their internal peace and social welfare, but threatens the general peace of the world,

Desiring to co-operate for defence against communistic disintegration, have agreed as follows:

Article I

The High Contracting States agree that they will mutually keep each other informed concerning the activities of the Communistic International, will confer upon the necessary measures of defence, and will carry out such measures in close co-operation.

Article II

The High Contracting States will jointly invite third States whose internal peace is menaced by the disintegrating work of the Communistic International, to adopt defensive measures in the spirit of the present Agreement or to participate in the present Agreement.

Article III

. . . The Agreement shall come into force on the day of its signature and shall remain in force for the term of five years. The High Contracting States will, in a reasonable time before the expiration of the said term, come to an understanding upon further manner of their cooperation. . . .

Supplementary Protocol to the
Agreement Guarding Against the Communistic International[2]

Berlin, November 25, 1936

On the occasion of the signature on this day of the Agreement guarding against the Communistic International the undersigned plenipotentiaries have agreed as follows:

a. The competent authorities of both High Contracting States will closely co-operate in the exchange of reports on the activities of the Communistic International and on measures of information and defence against the Communistic International.

b. The competent authorities of both High Contracting States will, within the framework of the existing law, take stringent measures against those who at home or abroad work on direct or indirect duty of the Communistic International or assist its disintegrating activities.

c. To facilitate the co-operation of the competent authorities of the two High Contracting States as set out in a) above, a standing committee shall be established. By this committee the further measures to be adopted in order to counter the disintegrating activities of the Communistic International shall be considered and conferred upon. . . .

Japan Explains Her Action

Tokyo, November 25, 1936[3]

1. Ever since its establishment the Communist International, or the so-called Comintern, with its headquarters at Moscow, for the purpose of destroying the national and social structures in every country in pursuance of its fundamental policy of world revolution, has been engaged in all sorts of activities, greatly menacing the peace of the world. At its Seventh Congress held in the summer of last year, the Comintern decided upon a policy of organizing a unified front with the Second [Socialist] International to oppose Fascism and imperialism, and at the same time made it plain that the future objectives of Comintern activities were to be Japan, Germany and Poland, etc; and it further resolved to support the Chinese communist armies in order to fight Japan. The actual operations carried on subsequently by the Comintern have become extremely ingenious, rendering them all the more dangerous. As to the extent to which the Comintern interferes with the internal affairs of all countries and exerts baneful influences on the well-being of the nations and the peace of the world, a glance at the present disturbances in Spain will be sufficient to convince anybody of its magnitude. At least those countries which lodged protests

with the Government of the Soviet Union at the time of the Comintern Congress must certainly have full cognizance of the harmfulness of Comintern activities.

2. The communist invasion has hitherto been more marked in the Orient, especially in China. Outer Mongolia and Sinkiang have already suffered from its calamitous effects while China Proper is now being subjected to the depredations of the communist armies. The activities of the Comintern in China have, as a matter of fact, notably increased in vigor since its Seventh Congress.

   In Manchukuo, also, the Comintern has been surreptitiously endeavoring through the Manchurian District Committee of the Chinese Communist Party to organize cells, to win over and instigate the bandits, and to direct the raids by partisan troops all over the country.

   In Japan, the extreme Leftist movement temporarily showed signs of decline after the Manchurian Incident. But since the Seventh Congress of the Comintern, the movement has again become energetic. It has crept into the channels of lawful agitation in conformance with the resolution of that Congress, and has launched a unified front movement to make it a basis for the revival of the communist movement.

3. The Japanese Government, who, in order to safeguard Japan's immutable national policy and insure the national security, and to maintain an everlasting peace in East Asia have pursued a clearcut and consistent policy toward the Comintern, find it necessary to take more rigorous measures of self-defense against its increased menace as stated above. The organization and the activities of the Comintern being of an international character, any program of counter action should necessarily be based upon international co-operation. Now Germany, ever since the establishment of the present regime in 1933, has put into execution drastic anti-communist policies. Last year at the Seventh Congress of the Comintern she was selected together with Japan as a special objective of Comintern operations. Thus Japan and Germany are placed in similar circumstances vis-á-vis the Comintern. Consequently the Japanese Government as the first step of their defensive undertaking conducted negotiations with Germany and concluded an agreement on November 25 to take effect immediately.

4. This agreement, the fundamental object of which is common defense against the destructive operations of the Comintern, contains provisions for the exchange of information regarding Comintern activities, for the consultation on, and the execution of, defensive measures and for the extension of joint invitations to third Powers. There is, besides, a supplementary Protocol stipulating in concrete terms the manners of executing the present agreement.

5. The Japanese Government are desirous of co-operating with as many Powers as possible for the purpose of perfecting their defensive

measures against the Comintern menace, but for that purpose alone. It should be pointed out that in connection with, or behind, this agreement there exists no special agreement whatsoever, and that the Japanese Government have no intention to form, or to join in, any special international bloc, for any other purpose and finally that the present agreement is not directed against the Soviet Union or any other specific country.

The United States Imposes Economic Controls

Adopting a policy of aid to China "short of war" after the fighting resumed in 1937, the Roosevelt Administration made loans to China, refused to invoke the Neutrality Act, and allowed Americans to fly as volunteers with the Chinese air force. While not invoking the Neutrality Act permitted continued American aid to China, Japan could also purchase critical supplies such as aviation gasoline and scrap metal, needed for the war effort in China.

In 1911 the United States and Japan had signed a commercial treaty, still in effect in 1937, that sanctioned trade between the two nations. Termination of that treaty would not automatically end the sale of goods to Japan, but it would be the first step in ending the steady movement of merchant ships to Japanese ports.

In July, 1939, the United States gave notice that the treaty would be terminated. Six months later, in accordance with the deadline established in the pact, treaty-sanctioned trade with Japan ended. In its place came a highly regulated system of licensing, based on action taken by the American government in July 1940, under which future trade would face growing restrictions and limitations that cut exports to Japan significantly.

The constant tightening of economic sanctions following termination of the commercial treaty presented Japan with a dilemma: either end the fighting in China and reach a settlement with the United States or take control of European colonies in the Southwest Pacific as a means of acquiring petroleum and other crucial resources. Unconvinced that the United States would commit itself to the defense of British, Dutch, or French colonies in Southeast Asia, Japan moved ahead with plans to secure those resources, through military means if necessary.

Abrogation of the 1911 Treaty of Commerce

The Secretary of State to the Japanese Ambassador (Horinouchi)[4]

Washington, July 26, 1939

Excellency: During recent years the Government of the United States has been examining the treaties of commerce and navigation in force between the United States and foreign countries with a view to determining what changes may need to be made toward better serving the purposes for which such treaties are concluded. In the course of this survey, the Government of the United States has come to the conclusion that the Treaty of Commerce and Navigation between the United States and Japan which was signed at Washington on February 21, 1911, contains provisions which need new consideration and with a view to better safeguarding and promoting American interests as new developments may require, the Government of the United States, acting in accordance with the procedure prescribed in Article XVII of the treaty under reference, gives notice hereby of its desire that this treaty be terminated, and, having thus given notice, will expect the treaty, together with its accompanying protocol, to expire six months from this date.

Cordell Hull

Export Controls Begin

Press Release Issued by the White House[5]

July 31, 1940

Col. R. L. Maxwell, Administrator of the Export Control, recommends, and the President approves, the issuance of the following announcement:

In the interests of the national defense the export of aviation gasoline is being limited to nations of the Western Hemisphere, except where such gasoline is required elsewhere for the operations of American-owned companies.

The Japanese Protest

The Japanese Embassy to the Department of State[6]

Washington, August 3, 1940

The Japanese Government has taken note of the Proclamation, dated July 26, 1940, by the President of the United States of America, for the administration of section 6 of the Act of Congress approved July 2, 1940, entitled

"An Act to expedite the strengthening of the national defense," and the Regulations, dated July 26, 1940, governing the exportation of articles and materials designated in the President's Proclamation of July 2, 1940, and the announcement of July 31 recommended by Colonel R. L. Maxwell, Administrator of Export Control. . . .

It is the understanding of the Japanese Government that the [July 31] announcement expresses the policy to be followed by the Government of the United States in applying the above mentioned Proclamations and Regulations to the export of aviation gasoline and that that policy, by limiting the export destinations, is tantamount to an embargo on aviation gasoline so far as countries outside the Western Hemisphere are concerned. As a country whose import of American aviation gasoline is of immense volume, Japan would bear the brunt of the virtual embargo. The resultant impression would be that Japan had been singled out for and subjected to discriminatory treatment.

While reserving all rights of further action, the Government of Japan wishes to protest against the policy of the Government of the United States set forth in the announcement under review.

America Explains

The Department of State to the Japanese Embassy[7]

Washington, August 9, 1940

Reference is made to the Japanese Ambassador's note of August 3, 1940 in regard to action taken by the Government of the United States . . . to restrict the export of aviation gasoline from the United States. . . .

The Government of the United States desires to state that the action under reference . . . is necessary in the interest of the national defense and that, accordingly, this Government considers a protest by any foreign government against that action to be unwarranted.

Export Controls Expanded

Press Release Issued by the White House[8]

September 26, 1940

The President has approved the early establishment of additional controls of the exportation of iron and steel scrap with a view to conserving the available supply to meet the rapidly expanding requirements of the defense program in this country.

Effective October 15, 1940 all outstanding balances of licenses which have been granted pursuant to the existing regulations of July 26, 1940 for the exportation of No. 1 heavy melting steel scrap will be revoked. On October 16, 1940 the exportation of all grades of iron and steel scrap will be placed under the licensing system.

Under the new regulations . . . licenses will be issued to permit shipments to the countries of the Western Hemisphere and Great Britain only.

Japan Doubts American Motives

The Japanese Embassy to the Department of State[9]

Washington, October 7, 1940

The Japanese Government has taken note of the regulations governing the exportation of iron and steel scrap, dated September 30, 1940 . . . and the announcement of September 26, 1940 to the effect that, under the new regulations, licenses will be issued to permit shipments to the countries of the Western Hemisphere and Great Britain only.

The above mentioned regulations . . . suggest that it was determined to be necessary in the interest of national defense to curtail the exportation of iron and steel scrap.

In view of the situation of iron and steel scrap markets, the supply and demand of these materials and the volume shipped to Japan, the Japanese Government finds it difficult to concede that this measure was motivated solely by the interest of national defense of the United States.

In the note of the Japanese Ambassador of August 3 the Japanese Government pointed out that the measure announced on July 26, 1940, in regard to the exportation of aviation gasoline, was tantamount to an export embargo as far as countries outside the Western Hemisphere were concerned. Compared to that announcement, the announcement under review may be said to have gone a step further toward discrimination by specifically excluding Great Britain from the virtual embargo.

In view of the fact that Japan has been for some years the principal buyer of American iron and steel scrap, the announcement of the administrative policy, as well as the regulations establishing [a] licensing system in iron and steel scrap cannot fail to be regarded as directed against Japan, and as such, to be an unfriendly act.

The Japanese Government hereby protests against the measures taken by the United States Government in connection with the exportation of iron and steel scrap.

A Warning from Japan

The Japanese Embassy to the Department of State[10]

Washington, October 8, 1940

Since iron and steel scrap classified as No. 1 heavy melting scrap was placed under export-licensing system on July 26, 1940, permission of the United States Government was obtained up to August 19 of the same year for 99 percent of applications for shipments to Japan.

In the light of this fact, the sudden enlargement of the iron and steel scrap licensing system to include all grades of these materials is hardly explicable from the standpoint of national defense, on which the regulation of September 30, 1940, is purported to be based.

The discriminatory feature of the announcement, that licenses will be issued to permit shipments to the countries of the Western Hemisphere and Great Britain only, has created a widespread impression in Japan that it was motivated by a desire to bring pressure upon her.

The fact that the majority of essential articles and materials that Japan desires to import from America is placed under licensing system is causing a feeling of tension among the people of Japan, who naturally presume that the system is intended to be a precursor of severance of economic relations between Japan and the United States.

In view of the high feeling in Japan it is apprehended that, in the event of continuation by the United States Government of the present attitude toward Japan in matters of trade restrictions, especially if it leads to the imposition of further measures of curtailment, further relations between Japan and the United States will be unpredictable.

It is a matter of course that the Governments of both Japan and the United States should endeavor as best they can to preclude such an eventuality. To this endeavor the Japanese Government will devote itself and trusts that it may have the full co-operation of the United States Government.

Hull Berates an Ambassador

Washington, October 8, 1940[11]

The Japanese Ambassador called at his request. He first expressed his regret at the unsatisfactory relations existing between our two countries at this time. I replied that, in my opinion, this was not the fault of the Ambassador and myself, who have been untiring in our efforts to promote and preserve satisfactory relations between the United States and Japan.

The Ambassador then said that he was instructed by his Government to hand me a note dated October 7, 1940 relative to our scrap iron and steel embargo which was recently proclaimed.

He read a statement in support of the note mentioned above.

I replied to the effect that I would see what sort of written reply, if any, might be called for.

I then said that I might at this time, and without delay, state that this Government at all times must determine for itself such internal questions as those material to our program of national defense, as we are doing in the instant case, and that it would be impossible for any country engaged in the serious and urgent undertaking of carrying out a program of national defense to allow every other outside nation to come in and pass upon the question of our needs of given commodities; that the embargo, as the Ambassador knows, applies to all nations except Great Britain and the Western Hemisphere. I remarked that for some years this Government had been criticized for not imposing numerous embargoes, primarily from the standpoint of safety and national defense and peace, and that it was only at the height of our national defense preparations that we were imposing a few embargoes on important commodities.

I said that it was really amazing for the Government of Japan, which has been violating in the most aggravating manner valuable American rights and interests throughout most of China, and is doing so in many instances every day, to question the fullest privilege of this Government from every standpoint to impose the proposed scrap iron and steel embargo, and that to go still further and call it an unfriendly act was still more amazing in the light of the conduct of the Japanese Government in disregarding all law, treaty obligations and other rights and privileges and the safety of Americans while it proceeded at the same time to seize territory by force to an ever-increasing extent. I stated that of all the countries with which I have had to deal during the past eight years, the Government of Japan has the least occasion or excuse to accuse this Government of an unfriendly act. I concluded with the statement that apparently the theory of the Japanese Government is for all other nations to acquiesce cheerfully in all injuries inflicted upon their citizens by the Japanese policy of force and conquest, accompanied by every sort of violence, unless they are to run the risk of being guilty of an unfriendly act.

The Ambassador again said that he very much regretted the serious differences between our two countries, but that he naturally hoped that trouble may yet be avoided. He added that any Japanese or any American must know that strife between the two countries would be extremely tragic for both alike. To this I replied that, of course, it would be exceedingly unfortunate for such occurrence to take place, but I added that my Government has been patient, extremely patient, and that the Ambassador will bear witness to the long and earnest efforts that he and I have made, and that I have made prior to his coming here, to promote and preserve friendly and satisfactory relations with Japan. I went on to say that we have stood for law and order and treaty observance and justice along with genuine friendliness between our two countries; that it was clear now, however, that those who are dominating the external policies of Japan are, as we here have believed for some years, bent on the conquest by force of all worthwhile territory in the Pacific Ocean area without limit as to extent in the South and in southern continental areas of that part of the world, and that we and all other nations are expected, as stated, to sit perfectly quiet and be cheerful and agreeable, but static, while most of Asia is Manchuria-ized, which would render practically impossible all reasonable or satisfactory relations so far as other nations are concerned; and that corresponding lower levels of existence would be the ultimate lot of the people of most of Asia. The least objection to or taking of issue with Japan with respect to the foregoing matters would be called an unfriendly act, and, as Prime Minister [Prince Fumimaro] Konoye said recently to the press, it would be the occasion for war so far as Japan was concerned. I added that, of course, if any one country is sufficiently desirous of trouble, it can always find any one of innumerable occasions to start such trouble. In brief, it is not left to the other country to participate in such decision.

The Ambassador undertook to repeat the old line of talk about how fair Japan proposed to be with respect to all rights and privileges of foreign nations within its conquered territory. He agreed that no purpose would be served now to go over the many conversations we must have had with respect to these matters. I held up the succession of injuries to American rights and interests in China whenever he referred to the scrap iron embargo.

I reiterated the view that it was unheard of for one country engaged in aggression and seizure of another country, contrary to all law and treaty provisions, to turn to a third peacefully disposed nation and seriously insist that it would be guilty of an unfriendly act if it should not cheerfully provide some of the necessary implements of war to aid the aggressor nation in carrying out its policy of invasion. I made it clear that it is the view of this Government that two nations, one in Europe and one in Asia, are undertaking to subjugate both of their respective areas of the world, and to place them on an international order and on a social basis resembling that of 750 years ago. In the face of this world movement, extending itself from day to day, peaceful and interested nations are to be held up to denunciation and threats if they dare to engage in any lawful acts or utterances in opposition to such wide movements of world conquest.

The Ambassador had little to say. He said virtually nothing in attempted extenuation except that his Government would expect everybody to receive considerate and fair treatment throughout the conquered areas. He emphasized equal treatment, and I replied that when the best interests of other nations in peace and law and order were being destroyed, it was not a matter of any concern as to whether there was discrimination between the nations which were victims of such movements.

Hull

America Finds "No Warrantable Basis" for Protest

The Department of State to the Japanese Embassy[12]

Washington, October 23, 1940

Reference is made to the note dated October 7, 1940, from the Japanese Embassy at Washington, in which objection is expressed by the Japanese Government to the regulations promulgated by the American Government on September 30, 1940, with regard to the exportation of iron and steel scrap, such objection being placed apparently on the ground that the restrictions to be effected by the regulations are discriminatory and are calculated to be injurious to Japan.

. . . It having been found by the appropriate agencies and authorities of this Government that the restrictions on exportation to be effected by the regulations under reference are necessary in the interest of national defense, the Government of the United States perceives no warrantable basis for a raising of question by any other government, in the circumstances—not of this Government's making—which prevail today in international relations, with regard to the considerations which necessitate the adoption by this Government of these measures of conservation.

Controls Extended Again

Press Release Issued by the Department of State[13]

December 10, 1940

The White House today, upon direction of the President, made public the following statement:

The President announced today that national-defense requirements for iron and steel have increased to such extent that it has become necessary to subject, as of December 30, 1940, iron ore, pig iron, ferro alloys, and certain iron and steel manufactures and semi-manufactures to the licensing requirement. Licenses will be granted for exports to the British Empire and the Western Hemisphere; and for the present, so far as the interests of the national defense permit, for exports to other destinations in quantities approximating usual or prewar exports.

Japan Protests, Again

The Japanese Embassy to the Department of State[14]

Washington, December 21, 1940

The Japanese Government has taken note of the Proclamation, dated December 10, 1940, by the President . . . governing the exportation of iron and steel . . . and of the "White House Announcement" of the same date. . . .

The enforcement of the measure ordered by the President in the Proclamation, especially when carried out in accordance with the policy as announced—that is the granting of licenses for exports exclusively to certain countries while subjecting exports to other countries to the considerations of "the interests of the national defense" and to arbitrary quantitative limitations—constitutes an instance of discriminatory treatment of countries in the latter category, of which Japan, in consideration of the volume of her importation in recent years of the specified commodities, would be one of those most gravely affected.

The Japanese Government, which has had occasion to file protests against discriminations embodied in previous Presidential Proclamations, regulations, and announcements of administrative policy governing the exportation of aviation gasoline and iron and steel scrap, by the Japanese Ambassador's notes of August 3, 1940 and October 8, 1940, respectively, is now constrained to protest, under similar circumstances and for similar reasons, against this fresh measure of discrimination reviewed in the above.

The United States Answers, Again

The Department of State to the Japanese Embassy[15]

Washington, January 7, 1941

Reference is made to the note . . . dated December 21, 1940, from the Japanese Embassy at Washington, in regard to restrictions recently placed on the exportation of iron and steel.

It is noted that the Embassy refers to its notes of August 3, 1940, and October 7[8?], 1940, in regard to the restrictions placed on the exportation of aviation gasoline and iron and steel scrap. The Embassy's attention is invited to the replies which the Department addressed to these notes on August 9, 1940, and October 23, 1940. The statements therein made concerning the interests of the national defense of the United States apply fully to the considerations raised in the Embassy's note under acknowledgment in regard to the recent restrictions on the export of iron and steel.

Japan Moves Into Indochina

Following the fall of France in June, 1940, Japan's new foreign minister, Yosuke Matsuoka, put pressure on French Indochina, an area of great importance to the Japanese on several grounds. It would give Japan another base from which to launch ground attacks on China, and from Indochina air fields Japanese planes would be in striking distance of supplies entering China via the Burma Road. In addition, Indochina would provide Japan with both food and resources badly needed in the war.

While many French colonies pledged loyalty to the anti-German, Free French government after France's defeat, Indochina was not in a position to do so. Colonial officials there adhered to the German-sponsored government at Vichy, France, which was not inclined to oppose Japanese designs in Southeast Asia.

Unable to resist the Japanese threat, French authorities first allowed Japanese observers into northern Indochina. Then, in September, the French were presented with a virtual ultimatum, one that they were in no position to reject. While some French army units did offer brief resistance, northern Indochina was soon occupied by the Japanese.

Hull Seeks Information

The Secretary of State to the Ambassador in Japan (Grew)[16]

Washington, September 3, 1940

At earliest moment possible, unless you perceive objection, please obtain further interview with Minister for Foreign Affairs. . . .

. . . Refer to the conversation you had on August 7 with the Minister and say to him that within the past few days reports from several sources have come to the Department of State to the effect that the Government of Japan has presented an ultimatum to the French authorities in Indochina on Japan's demands for permission to Japanese armed forces, for purposes of military operations against China, to pass through French territory and to use military bases and other facilities. The Government of the United States is reluctant to believe these reports, and it wishes to point out the unfortunate effect on American public opinion from the point of view of Japanese-American relations if these reports prove to be correct. Especially will this be true in view of statement which the press attributed on June 19 to a representative of the Japanese Foreign Office which said, in effect, that Japan attached importance to maintaining the *status quo* in French Indochina. . . .

Hull

Japan Gives Qualified Assurances

The Ambassador in Japan (Grew) to the Secretary of State[17]

Tokyo, September 4, 1940

. . . As the Minister was temporarily ill, I approached the Vice Minister for Foreign Affairs this afternoon on the subject of French Indochina in precise accord with your instructions.

The Vice Minister denied that he knew anything about an ultimatum, but he did not deny that armed forces of Japan did intend to seek passage through French Indochina. [He] said that the Japanese intention was a matter of military necessity; that there would be no permanent occupation of French territory; and that Japan would withdraw the forces in question as soon as the military necessity ceased to exist. I spoke with emphasis on the attitude of the American Government; likewise on Japan's expressed attitude toward maintaining the *status quo* in French Indochina, and on the deplorable effect which the execution of the stated intention of Japan's armed forces would have on American public opinion.

Shortly after my interview with the Vice Minister, similar representations were made by the British Ambassador, who received approximately the same reply.

Grew

Japan Acts with "Brotherly Love"

Memorandum by the Ambassador in Japan (Grew)[18]

Tokyo, September 14, 1940

. . . The Vice Minister asked me to call this afternoon and handed to me a penciled "oral statement" in the Japanese language in reply to my representations to the Foreign Minister on August 7 with regard to the reported Japanese demands on French Indochina. [He] said that he wished to apologize for the delay; that the Minister after our conversation on August 7 had directed that a reply be immediately formulated and that it was due to the change in Foreign Office personnel that this reply had somehow disappeared and had only now come to light. The Vice Minister's attempt to summarize the Japanese text in English was so inadequate that I said that I would prefer to study the text itself and to submit it to my Government before venturing to comment. Our translation of the statement follows:

"In a conversation on August 7, 1940, Your Excellency made reference to newspaper reports to the effect that the Imperial Government had at that time presented certain demands to the French Government regarding French Indochina and said that the American Government was concerned therewith. The Imperial Government, because of the necessity to construct a new order in East Asia, had theretofore carried out negotiations with regard to French Indochina, and on that basis has continued progressively with satisfactory local negotiations.

"In settling the China Incident, Japan seeks the firm preservation of a minimum right to existence; but in accomplishing this objective, however, Japan has been avoiding conquests and exploitation, and has been employing brotherly love, mutual existence and mutual prosperity as guiding principles. Japan has, so far as it does not interfere with the accomplishment of the above objective, been making efforts not to bring about undesirable changes to the *status quo.*

"Under the ever-changing conditions of today, past rules and norms rapidly become inapplicable to actual conditions. It is clear that, merely to adhere blindly to such rules and norms is not the way to stabilize world peace. Despite the fact that in the western hemisphere epoch-making changes are actually being made in the *status quo,* Japan has as yet expressed no opinion for or against those changes. It has to be pointed out that intrusion by the United States in an area which is so remote from that country as in this case brings about the same effect upon Japan's public opinion as the meddlesome attitudes of a third country toward the policy of the United States concerning third-power territories in the western hemisphere would bring about upon public opinion in the United States."

Joseph E. Grew

The United States Protests

Statement by the American Ambassador in Japan (Grew) to the Japanese Minister for Foreign Affairs (Matsuoka)[19]

Tokyo, September 19, 1940

My Government has instructed me to make the following observations in reply to the oral statement which was handed to me by the Vice Minister for Foreign Affairs on September 14.

It is the opinion of my Government that the *status quo* of a third country is seriously affected when one of two countries which is engaged in hostilities with another insists, in order to attack the other, upon the right of the use of airdromes and the right of passage for troops through the third country. In the light of the Japanese Government's announced desire that the *status quo* be maintained in the Pacific area there appears to be an inconsistency in connection with the stipulations by the Japanese Government.

The American Government urges upon all governments the employment of peaceful means only in their relations with all other governments and with all other regions. The attitude of my Government toward the unwarranted use of pressure in international relations is global.

Hull Hears a Rumor

The Secretary of State to the Ambassador in Japan (Grew)[20]

Washington, September 19, 1940

The Consul at Hanoi has informed the Department that the Japanese commanding general has presented demands to the Governor General of Indochina for occupation of Hanoi, Haiphong, and five airports by the armed forces of Japan. According to Mr. Reed, General Nishihara has stipulated that unless Japan's demands are accepted, invasion of French Indochina by Japanese armed forces will start on September 22 at 10 p.m.

Please try to see the Minister for Foreign Affairs at earliest moment possible; inform him of the report which the Department has received; and express to him, as under instructions from this Government, the great surprise of the Government of the United States that in the light of all the circumstances, among which is Japan's voluntary pledge previously expressed to maintain and to preserve the *status quo* in the Pacific area, the Japanese authorities in French Indochina should have taken action giving rise to this report. You will also say that the Government of the United States assumes that the report which it has received, if it is based on fact, reflects action taken locally exceeding the instructions of the Government of Japan, as was reputedly the case when a previous ultimatum was presented by Japanese military authorities.

Grew Confirms It

Memorandum by the Ambassador in Japan (Grew)[21]

Tokyo, September 20, 1940

An appointment was made with Mr. Matsuoka on the afternoon of September 20, after the Department's telegram had been received and decoded and I precisely acted upon the instructions of the Department.

Mr. Matsuoka in reply said that apart from some minor changes, the particulars of which were not mentioned, the reports are correct that an ultimatum had been presented to the Governor General of Indochina by General Nishihara. The new situation was then explained to be as follows, by the Minister:

The French Ambassador, under instructions of the French [Vichy] Government, and the Japanese Government on August 30 had signed an agreement in Tokyo. Provisions of the agreement were *inter alia* for the movement of troops of Japan through Indochina and the use temporarily of airports. The Governor General of Indochina was on September 6 ready to sign an agreement which would have implemented the agreement signed in Tokyo on August 30, but he refused for reasons not evident to the authorities of Japan and obstructed the implementation of the agreement signed in Tokyo. The Japanese Government felt obliged, although with reluctance, to ask the French Government whether the actions of the Governor General were subject to control by the French Government, since the Governor General continued to be uncooperative, and whether on the basis of the agreement signed in Tokyo the French Government was exhibiting good faith. The French Government said that it was, and as evidently the Governor General was not acting in good faith and as the Japanese authorities were aware that to foreign Consuls stationed in Indochina the Governor had boasted that he was using obstructive tactics, the Japanese ultimatum reported was necessarily presented.

The purpose of the measures taken was, said the Minister, to enable the Japanese forces to attack Chiang Kai-shek and to bring peace to China. As soon as hostilities have ceased, he said, the Japanese forces would be withdrawn at once; the integrity and sovereignty of Indochina would be accorded full respect, and as a consequence there would be no interference in East Asia with the *status quo*. The Minister said that he, Prince Konoye, and other Government members were representative of a minority opinion in Japan and that it was their determination that Japan should not oppress, exploit or interfere with other countries' integrity. He said that a struggle was taking place against extreme elements within the country on this issue. My interruption at this point was to the effect that clauses pertaining to commerce and economics in Indochina were within the scope of the agreement. No denial was made to my statement but I was assured that exploitation would not ensue.

The terms of the agreement between France and Japan signed on August 30 were confidential, said the Minister, and their divulgence by either of the signatories would nullify them. He said he could confidentially tell me, however, that France had broached the subject first and a request was made for a renewal of guarantees pertaining to the integrity of Indochina based on the agreement between France and Japan which was negotiated at approximately the same time as the Anglo-Japanese Alliance was concluded. He did not recall the exact date but said that the agreement was in effect and registered with the League of Nations. (This presumably is the agreement of June 10, 1907, between France and Japan.) The Minister was interrupted with my question as to what country's encroachments France desired guarantees against. Mr. Matsuoka said that this was a moot question. He went on then to say that permission had been asked by Japan for the movement of forces across Indochina and for the use temporarily of airports as "compensation" for complying with the French request. This information was given me in confidence, he emphasized, and its accuracy would of necessity be denied in event of publicity.

The Minister talked lengthily, but in spite of this and his illogical reasoning the meaning of his remarks is reported to the Department with all possible precision. The Minister upon the conclusion of his remarks left at once to fulfill another engagement and I could say only that if Japanese troops moved into Indochina my Government would regard it emphatically as an infringement of the *status quo* which the Japanese Government had already pledged to preserve, and that a further statement of the attitude of my Government was reserved until consideration had been given to my report. . . .

Grew

Hull Denounces the Occupation

Press Release Issued by the Department of State[22]

September 23, 1940

In response to inquiries at the press conference today, the Secretary of State said:

"Events are transpiring so rapidly in the Indochina situation that it is impossible to get a clear picture of the minute-to-minute developments. It seems obvious, however, that the *status quo* is being upset and that this is being achieved under duress. The position of the United States in disapproval and in deprecation of such procedures has repeatedly been stated."

This Government has not at any time or in any way approved the French concessions to Japan. The attitude of this Government toward developments in French Indochina is as expressed by the Secretary of State this morning and in previous public statements.

Japan Joins The Axis

Beginning in the mid-1930s various powers negotiated alliances, military or otherwise, that would place them in a favorable position in the event of war. The Rome-Berlin Axis (1936), the Anti-Comintern Pact (1936), and the Hitler-Stalin Pact (1939) foreshadowed a even more ominous agreement that was signed in September, 1940.

Within a few days after Japan's occupation of northern Indochina, Germany, Italy and Japan broadened the Anti-Comintern Pact and the Rome-Berlin Axis into a formal military alliance that seemed to divide the world into two major spheres of influence.

The United States, by this time committed to a policy of all-out aid to Britain and her remaining allies in the war against Germany, was particularly bothered by Article 3 of the pact. Would an American entry into the European war on the side of Britain be interpreted by the Japanese as invoking Axis obligations that required Japan to declare war on America? That concern would dominate Japanese-American relations for the next year.

The Tripartite Pact[23]

September 27, 1940

The Governments of Germany, Italy and Japan consider it the prerequisite of a lasting peace that every nation in the world shall receive the space to which it is entitled. They have, therefore, decided to stand by and co-operate with one another in their efforts in Greater East Asia and the regions of Europe respectively. In doing this it is their prime purpose to establish and maintain a new order of things, calculated to promote the mutual prosperity and welfare of the peoples concerned. It is furthermore the desire of the three Governments to extend co-operation to nations in other spheres of the world who are inclined to direct their efforts along lines similar to their own for the purpose of realizing their ultimate object, world peace. . . .

Article 1
Japan recognizes and respects the leadership of Germany and Italy in the establishment of a new order in Europe.

Article 2
Germany and Italy recognize and respect the leadership of Japan in the establishment of a new order in Greater East Asia.

Article 3
Germany, Italy, and Japan agree to co-operate in their efforts on aforesaid lines. They further undertake to assist one another with all political, economic, and military means, if one of the three Contracting Powers is attacked by a Power at present not involved in the European War or in the Chinese-Japanese conflict. . . .

Article 5

Germany, Italy, and Japan affirm that the above agreement affects in no way the political status existing at present between each of the three Contracting Parties and Soviet Russia.

Article 6

The present pact shall become valid immediately upon signature and shall remain in force for ten years from the date on which it becomes effective. In due time, before the expiration of the said term, the High Contracting Parties shall, at the request of any one of them, enter into negotiations for its renewal. . . .

Japan Defends the Axis Alliance

A Statement to the United States concerning the three-power alliance.[24]

October 5, 1940

The recent three-power alliance is not aimed at any particular country. If Japan, Germany and Italy unite, the probability of being attacked by another country is decreased, the spreading of world disorder may be prevented, and in this sense the alliance contributes to world peace. By this treaty Japan has further clarified its intention to establish a new order in greater East Asia including the South Seas.

The construction of a new order in East Asia means the construction of a new order under which Japan establishes the relationship of common existence and mutual prosperity with the peoples of each and every land in greater East Asia, that is East Asia including the South Seas. In a position of equality with every other country, Japan may freely carry on enterprises, trade and emigration in and to each and every land in greater East Asia and thereby be enabled to solve its population problem. This does not mean these areas are to be exploited and conquered, nor does it mean these areas are to be closed to the trade and enterprises of other countries. Japan has long tried to solve its population problem through emigration, trade and enterprises abroad, but the various countries of Europe and America have nullified Japan's reasonable and peaceful efforts concerning its population problem since these countries have turned back Japanese immigrants to their great territories and have obstructed trade and enterprise.

In the greater East Asia sphere of mutual prosperity, the endeavor is being made to abolish such unnatural restrictions on the free activities of mankind. It is expected that this endeavor will be accomplished insofar as possible through peaceful means and with the least possible undesirable change in the *status quo.*

Japan's policy toward China forms an important part of the above endeavor. However, owing to the lack of understanding on the part of some Chinese people and to the attitude taken by England and the United States in not recognizing Manchukuo, which gave rise to Chiang Kai-shek's hope of recovering Manchukuo, an unfortunate clash of arms broke out. This clash is, in fact, war and therefore it is impossible for the Japanese Army during its activities to avoid affecting rights and interests of the powers in China. This is particularly true when such rights and interests hinder the prosecution of Japan's war against China. Accordingly, if the effects upon these rights and interests are to be brought to an end, it is most desirable to encourage and promote peace between Japan and China. This fact notwithstanding the powers are not only checking Japan's actions through legalistic arguments and treaty pronouncements which have become inapplicable because of changing conditions, but are also oppressing Japan through such means as restriction on the exportation of important commodities to Japan and at the same time are giving positive aid to Japan's enemy, the Chiang Kai-shek regime. These actions spring from hidden motives to keep the Orient under conditions of disorder as long as possible and to consume Japan's natural strength. We must believe that these actions are not for the love of peace and are not for the purpose of protecting rights and interests. Japan concluded a defensive alliance with Germany and Italy for no other purpose than to resist such pressure from the powers, and there is not the slightest intention to proceed to attack another country. If the United States understands the aforementioned conditions and circumstances and Japan's intentions with regard to the establishment of a new order in East Asia, there will be no change whatever in the relationship between Japan and the United States following the conclusion of this treaty. Japan is determined to settle all pending questions and to promote and foster friendship with the United States.

Grew And Roosevelt On Japanese Expansion

During the decade that Joseph Grew had been the American Ambassador to Japan he had developed a strong affinity for the country and its people. The growing tension between his nation and the Japan he deeply loved was of immense concern to him. Grew recognized that powerful elements in the Japanese government were taking that nation down a path he could not support.

Expansionists, both civilian and military, were more often than not in command of the Japanese government. Grew deplored this and feared that eventually the two nations would be drawn into conflict. But he also saw hopeful signs among a more moderate group of officials, and he believed that, by cultivating them and offering an American policy that would strengthen their position in the Japanese government, a crisis might be avoided. However, by 1941 the moderates whom Grew so desperately hoped would rise to the occasion had largely been silenced by the growing power of expansionists.

From his post in Tokyo Grew sent to Washington numerous notes outlining his concern. Subservient to a fault, Grew constantly reminded Washington that his observations must be read in the context of his isolation thousands of miles from Washington and the events occurring in Europe. Perhaps, he suggested, he was too close to Japan to properly analyze American policy in the Far East in the light of the larger picture. Historians might later wonder if Grew had undercut his own correct assessment of Asian events by these disclaimers.

United States Ambassador (to Japan) Joseph Grew,
to President Roosevelt [25]

Tokyo, December 14, 1940

I would give a great deal to know your mind about Japan and all her works. It seems to me to be increasingly clear that we are bound to have a showdown some day, and the principal question at issue is whether it is to our advantage to have that showdown sooner or to have it later.

The chief factors in the problem would seem, from this angle, to be:

1. whether and when Britain is likely to win the European war;
2. whether our getting into war with Japan would so handicap our help to Britain in Europe as to make the difference to Britain between victory and defeat; and
3. to what extent our own policy in the Far East must be timed with our preparedness program and with respect to the relative strength of the American and the Japanese Navies now and later.

Those are questions which, with our limited information here, I am not qualified even approximately to answer.

From the Tokyo angle we see the picture roughly as follows:

After eight years of effort to build up something permanently constructive in American-Japanese relations, I find that diplomacy has been defeated by trends and forces utterly beyond its control, and that our work has been swept away as if by a typhoon with little or nothing remaining to show for it. Japan has become openly and unashamedly one of the predatory nations and part of a system which aims to wreck about everything that the United States stands for. Only insuperable obstacles will now prevent the Japanese from digging in permanently in China and from pushing the southward advance, with economic control as a preliminary to political domination in the areas marked down. Economic obstacles, such as may arise from American embargoes, will seriously handicap Japan in the long run, but meanwhile they tend to push the Japanese onward in a forlorn hope of making themselves economically self-sufficient.

History has shown that the pendulum in Japan is always swinging between extremist and moderate policies, but as things stand today we believe that the pendulum is more likely to swing further toward extremes than to reverse its direction. Konoye, and especially Matsuoka, will fall in due course, but under present circumstances no Japanese leader or group of leaders could reverse the expansionist program and hope to survive.

Our own policy of unhurried but of inexorable determination in meeting every Japanese step with some step of our own has been eminently wise, and that policy has sunk deep into Japanese consciousness. But while important elements among the Japanese people deplore the course which their leaders are taking, those elements are nevertheless inarticulate and powerless and are likely to remain so. Meanwhile the Germans here are working overtime to push Japan into war with us. I have told Matsuoka point-blank that his country is heading for disaster. He has at least seen that his efforts to intimidate us have fallen flat and have had an effect precisely the reverse of that intended.

It therefore appears that sooner or later, unless we are prepared . . . to withdraw bag and baggage from the entire sphere of "Greater East Asia including the South Seas" (which God forbid), we are bound eventually to come to a head-on clash with Japan. [Grew later clarified "clash," stating that it need not be a military clash, but could be economic in nature.]

A progressively firm policy on our part will entail inevitable risks—especially risks of sudden uncalculated strokes such as the sinking of the *Panay* which might inflame the American people—but in my opinion those risks are less in degree than the far greater future dangers which we would face if we were to follow a policy of *laissez-faire*.

In other words, the risks of not taking positive measures to maintain our future security are likely to be much greater than the risks of taking positive measures as the southward advance proceeds. So far as I am aware, the great majority of the American people are in a mood for vigorous action. The principal point at issue, as I see it, is not whether we must call a halt to the Japanese program, but when.

It is important constantly to bear in mind the fact that if we take measures "short of war" with no real intention to carry those measures to their final conclusion if necessary, such lack of intention will be all too obvious to the Japanese who will proceed undeterred, and even with greater incentive, on their way. Only if they become certain that we mean to fight if called upon to do so will our preliminary measures stand some chance of proving effective and of removing the necessity for war. . . .

If by such action we can bring about the eventual discrediting of Japan's present leaders, a regeneration of thought may ultimately take shape in this country, permitting the resumption of normal relations with us and leading to a readjustment of the whole Pacific problem.

In a nutshell that is about the way I regard the present and future situation. No doubt you have seen some of my telegrams which have tried to paint the picture as clearly as has been possible at this post where we have to fumble and grope for accurate information, simply because among the Japanese themselves the right hand often doesn't know what the left hand is doing. Their so-called "New Structure" is in an awful mess and the bickering and controversy that go on within the Government itself are past belief. Every new totalitarian step is clothed in some righteous-sounding slogan. This, indeed, is not the Japan that we have known and loved. . . .

Roosevelt to Grew[26]

Washington, January 21, 1941

I have given careful consideration to your letter of December 14.

. . . I find myself in decided agreement with your conclusions. . . .

. . . I believe that the fundamental proposition is that we must recognize that the hostilities in Europe, in Africa, and in Asia are all parts of a single world conflict. We must, consequently, recognize that our interests are menaced both in Europe and in the Far East. We are engaged in the task of defending our way of life and our vital national interests wherever they are seriously endangered. Our strategy of self-defense must be a global strategy which takes account of every front and takes advantage of every opportunity to contribute to our total security.

You [ask] . . . whether our getting into war with Japan would so handicap our help to Britain in Europe as to make the difference to Britain between victory and defeat. In this connection it seems to me that we must consider whether, if Japan should gain possession of the region of the Netherlands East Indies and the Malay Peninsula, the chances of England's winning in her struggle with Germany would not be decreased thereby. . . . The British need assistance along the lines of our generally established policies at many points, assistance which in the case of the Far East is certainly well within the realm of "possibility" so far as the capacity of the United States is concerned. Their defense strategy must in the nature of things be global. Our strategy of giving them assistance toward ensuring our own security must envisage both sending of supplies to England and helping to prevent a closing of channels of communication to and from various parts of the world, so that other important sources of supply will not be denied to the British and be added to the assets of the other side.

. . . I firmly believe . . . that the British, with our help, will be victorious in this [European] conflict. The conflict may well be long and we must bear in mind that when England is victorious she may not have left the strength that would be needed to bring about a rearrangement of such territorial changes in the western and southern Pacific as might occur during the course of the conflict if Japan is not kept within bounds. I judge from the remarks . . . that you, too, attach due importance to this aspect of the problem.

I am giving you my thoughts at this length because the problems which we face are so vast and so interrelated that any attempts even to state them compels one to think in terms of five continents and seven seas. . . .

The Japanese-Soviet Neutrality Treaty

Within the Japanese government in the spring of 1941 a struggle developed over whether Japan should move north, against the Soviet Union, or to the south in the direction of the Dutch East Indies. A move southward was essential from the standpoint of acquiring resources, most notably petroleum. While the sale of aviation gasoline to Japan had been severely restricted, lesser quality gasoline and crude oil were still available for export to Japan. But the Japanese were not sure how long that would last. Occupation of the oil producing areas of Southeast Asia would guarantee a ready supply and permit the continuation of the war in China, now jeopardized by the possibility of an oil embargo.

But should Japanese forces move southward, what would the Russians do? A war in China and a war against European colonies in the East Indies, especially one in which the United States might become involved, would leave Japan's northern flank exposed to a Soviet attack. Since the Russians had a nonaggression pact with Germany, they might feel free to launch a war against Japanese holdings in Manchuria, Korea, and northern China.

To the Russians, a nonaggression pact with Japan was especially desirable in the light of a possible war with Germany. Japan was already in the Axis Pact and a Russo-German War might force the Russians to fight on two fronts.

With these considerations in mind, both nations moved to neutralize the other in April 1941. Leading the move for a pact with

Russia was Yosuke Matsuoka, Foreign Minister in Prime Minister Fumimaro Konoye's cabinet.

The Neutrality Treaty

Pact on Neutrality between Union of Soviet Socialist Republics and Japan, and Accompanying Declaration[27]

Signed at Moscow, April 13, 1941

Article 1. Both high contracting parties undertake to maintain peaceful and friendly relations between each other and mutually to respect the territorial integrity and inviolability of the other contracting party.

Article 2. In the event one of the contracting parties becomes the object of military action on the part of another or several third powers the second contracting party will observe neutrality during the course of the entire conflict.

Article 3. The present pact becomes effective on day of its ratification by both contracting parties and remains valid during a period of five years. If one of the contracting parties does not denounce the pact one year before the expiration of its terms, it will be considered automatically extended for the next five years.

Article 4. The present pact is subject to ratification within the shortest possible period of time. The exchange of instruments of ratification shall take place in Tokyo also within the shortest period of time.

Declaration

In accordance with the spirit of the pact of neutrality concluded April 13, 1941, between the U. S. S. R. and Japan, the Government of the U. S. S. R. and the Government of Japan in the interest of securing peaceful and friendly relations between the two countries solemnly declare:

The U. S. S. R. undertakes to respect the territorial integrity and inviolability of Manchukuo, and Japan undertakes to respect the territorial integrity and inviolability of the Mongolian People's Republic.

Konoye Announces the Pact

The Ambassador in Japan (Grew) to the Secretary of State[28]

Tokyo, April 14, 1941

The following statement by Prime Minister Konoye was issued by the Board of Information last night:

"The Japanese Government some time ago made public both at home and abroad their unalterable determination, by concluding the tripartite pact among Japan, Germany and Italy to prevent a world-wide spread of war and to secure the peace of greater East Asia with that pact as the axis of the country's foreign policy. It goes without saying that, in order to realize such a purpose, it is essential that Japan and the Soviet Union, which are neighbors in the Far East, should strengthen their peaceful and friendly relation on a lasting basis, reinforcing thereby the spirit of the said pact of alliance. With this conviction, the Government has for some time been conducting negotiations with the Soviet Government with a view to bringing about a fundamental adjustment of Japan's relation with the Soviet Union. With the present visit to Moscow of the Foreign Minister, Mr. Yosuke Matsuoka, as a turning point, the conversations between the two Governments have made rapid progress, resulting in the signature to-day, April 13, of the pact of neutrality . . . which has just been announced. At the same time the joint declaration by the two countries has been issued through which Japan respects the territorial integrity and inviolability of the People's Republic of Mongolia and the Soviet Union respects the territorial integrity and inviolability of Manchukuo, thereby expecting to bring tranquility to the Manchukuo-Soviet and Manchukuo-Outer Mongolian borders.

"It is my belief that the present pact has an epoch-making significance in the relations between Japan and the Soviet Union and that it will greatly contribute toward the promotion of world peace. I have no doubt that the pact will serve as a basis for rapid solution in a concrete manner of various pending questions between the two countries."

Notes

1. *Foreign Relations: Japan,* II, 153–154.
2. *Ibid.,* II, 154–155.
3. *Ibid.,* II, 155–157.
4. U. S. Department of State, *Foreign Relations of the United States: 1939* (Washington, 1955), III, 558–559.
5. *Foreign Relations: Japan,* II, 218.
6. *Ibid.,* II, 218–219.
7. *Ibid.,* II, 219–220.
8. *Ibid.,* II, 222–223.
9. *Ibid.,* II, 223–224.
10. *Ibid.,* II, 224–225.

V

"PRELIMINARY CONVERSATIONS:" APRIL THROUGH JUNE, 1941

By the spring of 1941 both the United States and Japan desired to reach an agreement covering a broad list of items on which there had been conflict. At the instigation of private citizens from both countries, who had presented a preliminary proposal to the State Department on April 9, conversations were undertaken at Washington.

Japan sought American recognition of her paramount interest in China and American guarantees that resources vital to Japan's economic well-being would not be cut off. For their part, the American representatives insisted that four years of Japanese expansion into China would not mean the end of economic equality there. Furthermore, American diplomats wanted a commitment from Japan that there would be no further expansion of the Japanese Empire and that regions occupied in China and Indochina would be evacuated.

Also of great importance to the United States was the interpretation Japan would make of the Axis Alliance in the event the United States went to war against Germany. Washington was fearful that Japan would take advantage of America's Atlantic involvement to launch aggressive action in the Pacific. In connection with this, a major American reason for seeking the agreement was to permit reduction of Allied forces in the Pacific so that they could be concentrated in Europe. Japan's recently concluded neutrality pact with the Soviet Union also had a bearing on this.

From April through June 1941, draft and redraft of the proposed agreement moved back and forth between Tokyo and Washington. While on first reading the points presented in the original draft proposal might have seemed acceptable to both nations, sharp-eyed foreign office personnel in Tokyo and Washington found numerous passages that afforded opportunities for contradictory interpretations. Basic to the difficulty of reaching an agreement was whether the preliminary conversations should be limited to general principles, as Prime Minister Fumimaro Konoye urged, or concerned with specific details, as Secretary of State Hull insisted.

The Draft Treaty

Early in 1941 two prominent Catholic clergymen with strong ties to the Roosevelt Administration arranged a meeting with the President and Hull. They had recently returned from Japan where they had met with Japanese officials who, they claimed, were prepared to reach a settlement with the United States. Moderates in the Japanese government were ready to opt for peaceful economic penetration of Asia, rather than military action, provided that Japan could be assured of favorable economic relations with the west and that Japan's special interests in Asia be recognized. The moderates insisted that all negotiations must be secret, however, to prevent militaristic elements in Japan from frustrating the effort. Central to the success of the negotiations would be a summit conference, called by the two powers to announce the agreement in such a manner that it would be difficult for opponents in Japan to reject the settlement.

Roosevelt and Hull gave approval for the two clergymen, Bishop James Walsh and Father James Drought, to pursue their efforts privately. Working with two Japanese associates in Washington, who were closely connected to the Konoye government, Drought developed a draft treaty based on what he had learned while in Japan and what he knew about American policy. Over the next several weeks the draft went through various revisions, but no one in the American government actually participated in the writing of it. On April 9 the original draft was sent to the State Department.

Proposal presented to the Department of State
Through the Medium of Private American and Japanese Individuals
on April 9, 1941[1]

The Governments of the United States and of Japan accept joint responsibility for the initiation and conclusion of a general agreement, disposing the resumption of our traditional friendly relations.

Without reference to specific causes of recent estrangement, it is the sincere desire of both Governments that the incidents which led to the deterioration of amicable sentiment among our peoples should be prevented from recurrence and corrected in their unforeseen and unfortunate consequences.

It is our present hope that, by a joint effort, our nations may establish a just Peace in the Pacific; and by the rapid consummation of an *entente cordiale*, arrest, if not dispel, the tragic confusion that now threatens to engulf civilization.

For such decisive action, protracted negotiations would seem ill-suited and weakening. We, therefore, suggest that adequate instrumentalities should be developed for the realization of a general agreement which would bind, meanwhile, both governments in honor and in act.

It is our belief that such an understanding should comprise only the pivotal issues of urgency and not the accessory concerns which could be deliberated at a Conference and appropriately confirmed by our respective Governments.

We presume to anticipate that our Governments could achieve harmonious relations if certain situations and attitudes were clarified or improved: to wit:

1. The concepts of the United States and of Japan respecting international relations and the character of nations.
2. The attitudes of both governments toward the European War.
3. The relations of both nations toward the China Affair.
4. Naval, aerial and mercantile marine relations in the Pacific.
5. Commerce between both nations and their financial cooperation.
6. Economic activity of both nations in the Southwestern Pacific area.
7. The policies of both nations affecting political stabilization in the Pacific.

Accordingly, we have come to the following mutual understanding subject, of course, to modifications by the United States Government and subject to the official and final decision of the Government of Japan.

1. *The concepts of the United States and of Japan respecting international relations and the character of nations.*

   The Governments of the United States and of Japan might jointly acknowledge each other as equally sovereign states and contiguous Pacific powers.

   Both Governments assert the unanimity of their national policies as directed toward the foundation of a lasting peace and the inauguration of a new era of respectful confidence and cooperation among our peoples.

   Both Governments might declare that it is their traditional, and present, concept and conviction that nations and races compose, as members of a family, one household; each equally enjoying rights and admitting responsibilities with a mutuality of interests regulated by peaceful processes and directed to the pursuit of their moral and physical welfare, which they are bound to defend for themselves as they are bound not to destroy for others.

   Both Governments are firmly determined that their respective traditional concepts on the character of nations and the underlying moral principles of social order and national life will continue to be preserved and never transformed by foreign ideas or ideologies contrary to those moral principles and concepts.

2. *The attitudes of both Governments toward the European War.*

   The Government of Japan maintains that the purpose of its Axis Alliance was, and is, defensive and designed to prevent the extension of military grouping among nations not directly affected by the European War.

   The Government of Japan, with no intention of evading its existing treaty obligations, desires to declare that its military obligation under the Axis Alliance comes into force only when one of the parties of the Alliance is aggressively attacked by a power not at present involved in the European War.

   The Government of the United States maintains that its attitude toward the European War is, and will continue to be, determined by no aggressive alliance aimed to assist any one nation against another. The United States maintains that it is pledged to the hate of war, and accordingly, its attitude toward the European War is, and will continue to be, determined solely and exclusively by consideration of the protective defense of its own national welfare and security.

3. *The relations of both nations toward the China Affair.*

   The President of the United States, if the following terms are approved by His Excellency and guaranteed by the Government of Japan, might request the Chiang-Kai-Chek regime to negotiate peace with Japan.

a. Independence of China
b. Withdrawal of Japanese troops from Chinese territory, in accordance with an agreement to be reached between Japan and China
c. No acquisition of Chinese territory
d. No imposition of indemnities
e. Resumption of the "Open Door"; the interpretation and application of which shall be agreed upon at some future, convenient time between the United States and Japan
f. Coalescence of the Governments of Chiang-Kai-Chek and of Wang-Ching-Wei [The Chinese government at Nanking, recognized by Japan]
g. No large-scale or concentrated immigration of Japanese into Chinese territory
h. Recognition of Manchukuo

With the acceptance by the Chiang-Kai-Chek regime of the aforementioned Presidential request, the Japanese Government shall commence direct peace negotiations with the newly coalesced Chinese Government, or constituent elements thereof.

The Government of Japan shall submit to the Chinese concrete terms of peace, within the limits of aforesaid general terms and along the lines of neighborly friendship, joint defense against communistic activities and economic cooperation.

Should the Chiang-Kai-Chek regime reject the request of President Roosevelt, the United States Government shall discontinue assistance to the Chinese.

4. *Naval, aerial and mercantile marine relations in the Pacific.*
    a. As both the Americans and the Japanese are desirous of maintaining the peace in the Pacific, they shall not resort to such disposition of their naval forces and aerial forces as to menace each other. Detailed, concrete agreement thereof shall be left for determination at the proposed joint Conference.
    b. At the conclusion of the projected Conference, each nation might despatch a courtesy naval squadron to visit the country of the other and signalize the new era of Peace in the Pacific.
    c. With the first ray of hope for the settlement of China affairs, the Japanese Government will agree, if desired, to use their good offices to release for contract by Americans certain percentage of their total tonnage of merchant vessels, chiefly for the Pacific service, so soon as they can be released from their present commitments. The amount of such tonnage shall be determined at the Conference.

5. *Commerce between both nations and their financial cooperation.*
    When official approbation to the present understanding has been given by both Governments, the United States and Japan shall assure

each other to mutually supply such commodities as are respectively available or required by either of them. Both governments further consent to take necessary steps to the resumption of normal trade relations as formerly established under the Treaty of Navigation and Commerce between the United States and Japan. If a new commercial treaty is desired by both governments, it could be elaborated at the proposed conference and concluded in accordance with usual procedure.

For the advancement of economic cooperation between both nations, it is suggested that the United States extend to Japan a gold credit in amounts sufficient to foster trade and industrial development directed to the betterment of Far Eastern economic conditions and to the sustained economic cooperation of the Governments of the United States and of Japan.

6. *Economic activity of both nations in the Southwestern Pacific area.*
On the pledged basis of guarantee that Japanese activities in the Southwestern Pacific area shall be carried on by peaceful means, without resorting to arms, American cooperation and support shall be given in the production and procurement of natural resources (such as oil, rubber, tin, nickel) which Japan needs.

7. *The policies of both nations affecting political stabilization in the Pacific.*
   a. The Governments of the United States and of Japan will not acquiesce in the future transfer of territories or the relegation of existing States within the Far East and in the Southwestern Pacific area to any European Power.
   b. The Governments of the United States and of Japan jointly guarantee the independence of the Philippine Islands and will consider means to come to their assistance in the event of unprovoked aggression by any third Power.
   c. The Government of Japan requests the friendly and diplomatic assistance of the Government of the United States for the removal of Hongkong and Singapore as doorways to further political encroachment by the British in the Far East.
   d. Japanese Immigration to the United States and to the Southwestern Pacific area shall receive amicable consideration—on a basis of equality with other nationals and freedom from discrimination.

Conference
a. It is suggested that a Conference between Delegates of the United States and of Japan be held at Honolulu and that this Conference be opened for the United States by President Roosevelt and for Japan by Prince Konoye. The delegates could number less than five each, exclusive of experts, clerks, etc.
b. There shall be no foreign observers at the Conference.

c. This Conference could be held as soon as possible (May, 1941) after the present understanding has been reached.

d. The agenda of the Conference would not include a reconsideration of the present understanding but would direct its effort to the specification of the prearranged agenda and drafting of instruments to effectuate the understanding. The precise agenda could be determined upon by mutual agreement between both governments.

Addendum

The present understanding shall be kept as a confidential memorandum between the Governments of the United States and of Japan.

The scope, character and timing of the announcement of this understanding will be agreed upon by both Governments.

Japan Offers Her First Draft

Through the rest of April and into May the two governments worked with the April 9 draft. Ambassador Kichisaburo Nomura, who had only recently arrived in Washington, sent the draft document to Tokyo, where it was revised by the foreign office and returned to the United States in mid-May. The first Japanese draft revealed certain areas of disagreement with the rough draft written by Drought and his Japanese associates, but it paralleled the document drawn up by the private citizens in most respects.

Only significant deviations from the April 9 draft are reprinted below. For clarity, sections have been renumbered to correspond to the April 9 draft and have been rearranged.

Presented by Ambassador Nomura to Secretary of State Hull, May 12, 1941.[2]

... Both Governments presume to anticipate that they could achieve harmonious relations if certain situations and attitudes were clarified or improved, to wit:

1. The concepts of the United States and of Japan respecting international relations and the character of nations.
2. The attitude of both Governments toward the European War.
3. The relations of both nations toward the China Affair.
[4. Japan's note omitted "Naval relations ... ," item 4 in the April 9 list.]
5. Commerce between both nations.
6. Economic activity of both nations in the Southwestern Pacific area.

7. The policies of both nations affecting political stabilization in the Pacific area.

Accordingly, we have come to the following mutual understanding: . . .

2. *The attitude of both Governments toward the European War.*

The Governments of the United States and Japan make it their common aim to bring about the world peace; they shall therefore jointly endeavor not only to prevent further extension of the European War but also speedily to restore peace in Europe.

The Government of Japan maintains that its alliance with the Axis Powers was, and is, defensive and designed to prevent the nations which are not at present directly affected by the European War from engaging in it.

The Government of Japan maintains that its obligations of military assistance under the Tripartite Pact between Japan, Germany and Italy will be applied in accordance with the stipulation of Article 3 of said Pact.

The Government of the United States maintains that its attitude toward the European War is, and will continue to be, directed by no such aggressive measures as to assist any one nation against another. The United States maintains that it is pledged to the hate of war, and accordingly, its attitude toward the European War is, and will continue to be, determined solely and exclusively by considerations of the protective defense of its own national welfare and security.

*Oral Explanation**

Actually the meaning of this . . . is virtually unchanged but we desire to make it clearer by specifying a reference to the Pact. As long as Japan is a member of the Tripartite Pact, such stipulation as is mentioned in the Understanding seems unnecessary.

If we must have any stipulation at all, in addition, it would be important to have one which would clarify the relationship of this Understanding to the aforementioned Pact. . . .

3. *The relations of both nations toward the China Affair.*

The Government of the United States, acknowledging the three principles as enunciated in the Konoe [Konoye] Statement and the principles set forth on the basis of the said three principles in the treaty with the Nanking Government as well as in the Joint Declaration of Japan, Manchoukuo and China and relying upon the policy of the Japanese Government to establish a relationship of neighborly friendship with China, shall forthwith request the Chiang Kai-shek regime to negotiate peace with Japan.

---

* Each *oral explanation* was to explain changes that Japan made in the original draft.

Oral Explanation

The terms for China-Japan peace as proposed in the original Understanding differ in no substantial way from those herein affirmed as the "principles of Konoe." Practically, the one can be used to explain the other.

We should obtain an understanding, in a separate and secret document, that the United States would discontinue her assistance to the Chiang Kai-shek regime if Chiang Kai-shek does not accept the advice of the United States that he enter into negotiations for peace.

If, for any reason, the United States finds it impossible to sign a document, a definite pledge by some highest authorities will suffice.

The three principles of Prince Konoe as referred to in this paragraph are:

1. Neighborly friendship;
2. Joint defense against communism;
3. economic cooperation—by which Japan does not intend to exercise economic monopoly in China nor to demand of China a limitation on the interests of Third Powers.

The following are implied in the aforesaid principles:

1. Mutual respect of sovereignty and territories;
2. Mutual respect for the inherent characteristics of each nation cooperating as good neighbors and forming a Far Eastern nucleus contributing to world peace;
3. Withdrawal of Japanese troops from Chinese territory in accordance with an agreement to be concluded between Japan and China;
4. No annexation, no indemnities;
5. Independence of Manchoukuo.

The stipulation regarding large-scale immigration to China has been deleted because it might give an impression, maybe a mistaken impression, to the Japanese people who have been offended by the past immigration legislation of the United States, that America is now taking a dictating attitude even toward the question of Japanese immigration in China.

Actually, the true meaning and purpose of this stipulation is fully understood and accepted by the Japanese Government. . . .

4. *Naval, Aerial and Mercantile Marine Relations.*

Oral Explanation

a. and c. of this section have been deleted not because of disagreement but because it would be more practical, and possible, to determine the disposition of naval forces and mercantile marine after an understanding has been reached and relations between our two countries improved; and after our present China commitments are eliminated. Then we will know the actual situation and can act accordingly.

Courtesy visit of naval squadrons. This proposal, 4b, might better be made a subject of a separate memorandum. Particular care must be taken as to the timing, manner and scope of carrying out such a gesture. . . .

6. *Economic activity of both nations in the Southwestern Pacific area.*
  Having in view that the Japanese expansion in the direction of the Southwestern Pacific area is declared to be of peaceful nature, American cooperation shall be given in the production and procurement of natural resources (such as oil, rubber, tin, nickel) which Japan needs.

Oral Explanation
  The words, in the [April 9] first paragraph, "without resorting to arms," have been deleted as inappropriate and unnecessarily critical. Actually, the peaceful policy of the Japanese Government has been made clear on many occasions in various statements made both by the Premier and the Foreign Minister. . . .

7. *The policies of both nations affecting political stabilization in the Pacific area.*
  a. The Government of the United States and Japan jointly guarantee the independence of the Philippine Islands on the condition that the Philippine Islands shall maintain a status of permanent neutrality. The Japanese subjects shall not be subject to any discriminatory treatment.
  b. Japanese immigration to the United States shall receive amicable consideration—on a basis of equality with other nations and freedom from discrimination.
    [The Japanese draft, without oral explanation, omitted reference to Hong Kong and Singapore.]

Oral Explanation
  As the paragraph a. [referring to April 9 draft statement on colonization in the Far East or the Southwestern Pacific] implying military and treaty obligations would require, for its enactment, such a complicated legislative procedure in both countries, we consider it inappropriate to include this in the present Understanding.
  Paragraph b. regarding the independence of the Philippine Islands has been altered for the same reason.
  . . . The words "and to the Southwestern Pacific Area" [regarding Japanese immigration] have been omitted because such questions should be settled, as necessity arises, through direct negotiation with the authorities in the Southwestern areas by the Government of the United States and of Japan respectively.

Conference

  The stipulation for holding a Conference has been deleted. We consider that it would be better to arrange, by an exchange of letters, that a conference between the President and the Premier or between suitable representatives of theirs will be considered when both the United States and Japan deem it useful to hold such a conference after taking into due consideration the effect resulting from the present Understanding.

The United States Responds

In May and June Hull and Nomura held numerous secret meetings to iron out differences. Hull wanted detailed, firm commitments from Japan on all the major issues so that nothing could be left to interpretation. The Japanese were more interested in getting general agreements in the draft, leaving final details to the conference that was expected to follow the drafting of the treaty.

During this time negotiations were left largely to Hull. Others with an interest in the subject, such as Henry Stimson, former Secretary of State and now Secretary of War, and Frank Knox, Secretary of the Navy, were not invited to participate in the revision of the draft. Nor were Under Secretary of State Sumner Welles, a moderate, or the Far Eastern expert in the Department, Stanley Hornbeck, who called for a hard-line against Japan, involved.

On May 31 the first American draft was presented to Nomura in Washington. By this time it was clear that numerous lesser issues could be easily disposed of but several fundamental differences remained before the identic notes that Drought believed must be forthcoming could be agreed to.

American Draft Proposal*

Handed to the Japanese Ambassador (Nomura) on May 31, 1941[3]

Unofficial, Exploratory and Without Commitment

... Both Governments presume to anticipate that they could achieve harmonious relations if certain situations and attitudes were clarified or improved; to wit:

1. The concepts of the United States and of Japan respecting international relations and the character of nations.
2. The attitudes of both Governments toward the European war.
3. Action toward a peaceful settlement between China and Japan.
[4. The American note also omitted the "Naval relations . . . " section.]
5. Commerce between both nations.
6. Economic activity of both nations in the Pacific area.
7. The policies of both nations affecting political stabilization in the Pacific area.

---

* Only significant deviations from the April 9 draft are reprinted here. For clarity, sections have been rearranged.

8. Neutralization of the Philippine Islands.

Accordingly, the Government of the United States and the Government of Japan have come to the following mutual understanding and declaration of policy: . . .

 2. *The attitudes of both Governments toward the European war.*

The Government of Japan maintains that the purpose of the Tripartite Pact was, and is, defensive and is designed to prevent the participation of nations in the European war not at present involved in it. Obviously, the provisions of the Pact do not apply to involvement through acts of self-defense.

The Government of the United States maintains that its attitude toward the European hostilities is and will continue to be determined solely and exclusively by considerations of protection and self-defense: its national security and the defense thereof.

Oral Explanation

The first paragraph of the Japanese draft has been omitted in order to avoid any implication of inconsistency with statements made by the President to the effect that the present is not an opportune time for the American Government to endeavor to bring about peace in Europe.

To the second paragraph of the Japanese draft a new sentence has been added to emphasize the aspect of self-defense.

The third paragraph has been omitted in-as-much as the text of the Tripartite Pact has been published and no purpose would appear to be served by express reference to any of its provisions.

The fourth paragraph of the Japanese draft has been revised to emphasize the protective and self-defense character of the attitude of the United States toward the European hostilities.

A statement in the Annex and Supplement [omitted here] on the part of the Government of the United States contains an elaboration of this Government's viewpoints toward the military movement of conquest inaugurated by Chancellor Hitler.

 3. *Action toward a peaceful settlement between China and Japan.*

The Japanese Government having communicated to the Government of the United States the general terms within the framework of which the Japanese Government will propose the negotiation of a peaceful settlement with the Chinese government, which terms are declared by the Japanese Government to be in harmony with the Konoe principles regarding neighborly friendship and mutual respect of sovereignty and territories and with the practical application of those principles, the President of the United States will suggest to the Government of China that the Government of China and the Government of Japan enter into a negotiation on a basis mutually advantageous and acceptable for a termination of hostilities and resumption of peaceful relations.

Note: (The foregoing . . . Section . . . is subject to further discussion of the question of cooperative defense against communistic activities, including the stationing of Japanese troops in Chinese territory.)

Oral Explanation

As already stated, the title has been altered to describe more accurately the contents.

The statement in the Japanese draft has been rewritten to keep the underlying purport and at the same time to avert raising questions which do not seem fundamental to the basic subject and which are controversial in character and might present serious difficulties from the point of view of the United States.

. . . In addition, point numbered three in regard to economic cooperation has been rephrased so as to make it clear that China and Japan intend to follow in their economic relations the principle of non-discrimination in international commercial relations, a principle to which it is understood the Japanese Government and the Chinese Government have long subscribed and which principle forms the foundation of the commercial policy of the United States. As it is assumed that the term "troops" . . . is meant to include all armed forces, the language of this point has been slightly rephrased to avoid possible ambiguity.

As already stated, the question relating to communistic activities, including the stationing of Japanese troops in Chinese territory, is subject to further discussion. . . .

The basic terms [for peace in China] are as follows:
a. Neighborly friendship.
b. (Cooperative defense against injurious communistic activities— including the stationing of Japanese troops in Chinese territory.) Subject to further discussion.
c. Economic cooperation—by which China and Japan will proceed on the basis of nondiscrimination in international commercial relations.
d. Mutual respect of sovereignty and territories.
e. Mutual respect for the inherent characteristics of each nation cooperating as good neighbors and forming a Far Eastern nucleu' contributing to world peace.
f. Withdrawal of Japanese military and naval forces from Chir territory and Chinese waters as promptly as possible and ' cordance with an agreement to be concluded between Jap China.
g. No annexation.
h. No indemnities.
i. Amicable negotiation in regard to Manchoukuo. . .

7. *The policies of both nations affecting political stabilization in the Pacific area.*
   The Japanese Government and the Government of the United
   States declare that the controlling policy underlying this understanding is peace in the Pacific area; that it is their fundamental purpose,
   through cooperative effort, to contribute to the maintenance and the
   preservation of peace in the Pacific area, and that neither has territorial designs in the area mentioned.

Oral Explanation
   This section has been revised to make it consist of a clear-cut statement of the fundamental purpose of the understanding. The thought in
mind is to give emphasis to this purpose so that the document may speak
for itself on this all-important subject.
   The statement of fundamental purpose has been assigned a section by
itself in order that it may gain added emphasis.
   The statement in the Japanese draft in regard to the Philippine Islands
has been dealt with in a new section. . . .
   The statement in regard to Japanese immigration has been omitted in
view of the established position of the United States that the question of
immigration is a domestic matter. For that reason, to attempt to include
a statement on this subject would stand in the way of the underlying purposes of the agreement.

8. *Neutralization of the Philippine Islands.*
   The Government of Japan declares its willingness to enter at such
   times as the Government of the United States may desire into negotiation with the Government of the United States with a view to the
   conclusion of a treaty for the neutralization of the Philippine Islands,
   when Philippine independence shall have been achieved.

Draft Proposals: Round Two

In mid-June the final drafts prepared by the two governments in
the current set of negotiations were exchanged. While on the sur-
face it appeared that both nations were very close to agreement and
ʾad made important concessions, problems still remained. Hull
ʾnd it necessary to raise several thorny questions in the Ameri-
ʾraft regarding Japanese economic activity in the Far East. He
veɽo concerned about Japan's attitude toward American inter-
Uniteᴙ the European war, though the Japanese had assured the
Axis Allᴛes in every way possible (except a withdrawal from the
ᵐatically tᴙᵉ) that American entry into that war would not auto-
ʾer Japanese obligations under the pact.

Despite these difficulties, there was room for optimism about the outcome of the preliminary conversations. By the end of June, however, a cycle of events had begun that would preclude successful negotiations between the two countries.

Draft Document Received Informally
From the Associates of the Japanese Ambassador (Nomura)
on June 15, 1941[4]

The Governments of the United States and of Japan accept joint responsibility for the initiation and conclusion of a general agreement of understanding as expressed in a joint declaration for the resumption of traditionally friendly relations.

Without reference to specific causes of recent estrangement, it is the sincere desire of both Governments that the incidents which led to the deterioration of amicable sentiment between their countries should be prevented from recurrence and corrected in their unforeseen and unfortunate consequences.

It is our earnest hope that, by a cooperative effort, the United States and Japan may contribute effectively toward the establishment and preservation of peace in the Pacific area and, by the rapid consummation of an amicable understanding, encourage world peace and arrest, if not dispel, the tragic confusion that now threatens to engulf civilization.

For such decisive action, protracted negotiations would seem ill-suited and weakening. Both Governments, therefore, desire that adequate instrumentalities should be developed for the realization of a general understanding which would bind, meanwhile, both Governments in honor and in act.

It is the belief of the two Governments that such an understanding should comprise only the pivotal issues of urgency and not the accessory concerns which could be deliberated at a Conference.

Both Governments presume to anticipate that they could achieve harmonious relations if certain situations and attitudes were clarified or improved; to wit:

1. The concepts of the United States and of Japan respecting the international relations and the character of nations.
2. The attitudes of both Governments toward the European war.
3. Action toward a peaceful settlement between China and Japan.
4. Commerce between both nations.
5. Economic activity of both nations in the Pacific area.
6. The policies of both nations affecting political stabilization in the Pacific area.
7. Neutralization of the Philippine Islands.

Accordingly, the Government of the United States and the Government of Japan have come to the following mutual understanding and declaration of policy:

1. *The concepts of the United States and of Japan respecting international relations and the character of nations.*

    Both Governments affirm that their national policies are directed toward the foundation of a lasting peace and the inauguration of a new era of reciprocal confidence and cooperation between our peoples.

    Both Governments declare that it is their traditional, and present, concept and conviction that nations and races compose, as members of a family, one household living under the ideal of universal concord through justice and equity; each equally enjoying rights and admitting responsibilities with a mutuality of interests regulated by peaceful processes and directed to the pursuit of their moral and physical welfare, which they are bound to defend for themselves as they are bound not to destroy for others; they further admit their responsibilities to oppose the oppression or exploitation of other peoples.

    Both Governments are firmly determined that their respective traditional concepts on the character of nations and the underlying moral principles of social order and national life will continue to be preserved and never transformed by foreign ideas or ideologies contrary to those moral principles and concepts.

2. *The attitudes of both Governments toward the European war.*

    The Government of Japan maintains that the purpose of the Tripartite Pact was, and is, defensive and is designed to prevent the participation of nations in the European war not at present involved in it.

    The Government of the United States maintains that its attitude toward the European hostilities is and will continue to be determined solely and exclusively by considerations of protection and self-defense: its national security and the defense thereof.

3. *Action toward a peaceful settlement between Japan and China.*

    The Government of Japan having declared that the general terms, within the framework of which the Government of Japan will propose the negotiation of a peaceful settlement of the China Affair, are implied in the Konoe principles and in the practical application of those principles, the President of the United States, relying upon the policy of the Government of Japan to establish a relation of neighborly friendship with China, will suggest to the Government at Chungking that it enter with the Government of Japan into a negotiation for a termination of hostilities and resumption of peaceful relations.

4. *Commerce between both nations.*

When official approbation to the present understanding has been given by both Governments, the United States and Japan shall assure each other mutually to supply such commodities as are, respectively, available and required by either of them. Both Governments further consent to take necessary steps to resume normal trade relations as formerly established under the Treaty of Commerce and Navigation between the United States and Japan. If a new commercial treaty is desired by both Governments, it would be negotiated as soon as possible and be concluded in accordance with usual procedures.

5. *Economic activity of both nations in the Pacific area.*

On the basis of mutual pledges hereby given that Japanese activity and American activity in the Pacific area shall be carried on by peaceful means and in conformity with the principle of non-discrimination in international commercial relations, the Japanese Government and the Government of the United States agree to cooperate each with the other toward obtaining non-discriminatory access by Japan and by the United States to commercial supplies of natural resources (such as oil, rubber, tin, nickel) which each country needs for the safeguarding and development of its own economy.

6. *The policies of both nations affecting political stabilization in the Pacific area.*

Both Governments declare that the controlling policy underlying this understanding is peace in the Pacific area; that it is their fundamental purpose, through cooperative efforts, to contribute to the maintenance and the preservation of peace in the Pacific area; and that neither has territorial designs in the area mentioned.

7. *Neutralization of the Philippine Islands.*

The Government of Japan declares its willingness to enter at such time as the Government of the United States may desire into negotiation with the Government of the United States with a view to the conclusion of a treaty for the neutralization of the Philippine Islands, when Philippine independence shall have been achieved.

Annex and Supplement*
on the Part of the Government of the United States

4. *Commerce between both nations.*

It is understood that during the present international emergency Japan and the United States each shall permit export to the other of commodities in amounts up to the figures of usual or pre-war trade, except, in the case of each, commodities which it needs for its own

---

* Note: The associates of Ambassador Nomura enclosed this Annex and Supplement.

purposes of security and self-defense. These limitations are mentioned to clarify the obligations of each Government. They are not intended as restrictions against either Government; and, it is understood, that both Governments will apply such regulations in the spirit dominating relations with friendly nations.

Draft Proposal
Handed by the Secretary of State
to the Japanese Ambassador (Nomura) on June 21, 1941[5]

Unofficial, Exploratory and Without Commitment. . . .

2. *The attitudes of both Governments toward the European war.*
  The Government of Japan maintains that the purpose of the Tripartite Pact was, and is, defensive and is designed to contribute to the prevention of an unprovoked extension of the European war. . . .

Annex

Suggested exchange of letters between the Secretary of State and the Japanese Ambassador

The Secretary of State to the Japanese Ambassador:
Excellency: In Section II of the Joint Declaration which was entered into today on behalf of our two Governments, statements are made with regard to the attitudes of the two Governments toward the European war. During the informal conversations which resulted in the conclusion of this Joint Declaration I explained to you on a number of occasions the attitude and policy of the Government of the United States toward the hostilities in Europe and I pointed out that this attitude and policy were based on the inalienable right of self-defense. I called special attention to an address which I delivered on April 24 setting forth fully the position of this Government upon this subject.

I am sure that you are fully cognizant of this Government's attitude toward the European war but in order that there may be no misunderstanding I am again referring to the subject. I shall be glad to receive from you confirmation by the Government of Japan that, with regard to the measures which this nation may be forced to adopt in defense of its own security, which have been set forth as indicated, the Government of Japan is not under any commitment which would require Japan to take any action contrary to or destructive of the fundamental objective of the present agreement, to establish and to preserve peace in the Pacific area. . . .

The Japanese Ambassador to the Secretary of State:
Excellency: I have received your letter of June—.

I wish to state that my Government is fully aware of the attitude of the Government of the United States toward the hostilities in Europe as explained to me by you during our recent conversations and as set forth in your address of April 24. I did not fail to report to my Government the policy of the Government of the United States as it had been explained to me, and I may assure you that my Government understands and appreciates the attitude and position of the Government of the United States with regard to the European war.

I wish also to assure you that the Government of Japan, with regard to the measures which the Government of the United States may be forced to adopt in defense of its own security, is not under any commitment requiring Japan to take any action contrary to or destructive of the fundamental objective of the present agreement.

The Government of Japan, fully cognizant of its responsiblities freely assumed by the conclusion of this agreement, is determined to take no action inimical to the establishment and preservation of peace in the Pacific area. . . .

3. *Action toward a peaceful settlement between China and Japan.*

The Japanese Government having communicated to the Government of the United States the general terms within the framework of which the Japanese Government will propose the negotiation of a peaceful settlement with the Chinese Government, which terms are declared by the Japanese Government to be in harmony with the Konoe principles regarding neighborly friendship and mutual respect of sovereignty and territories and with the practical application of those principles, the President of the United States will suggest to the Government of China that the Government of China and the Government of Japan enter into a negotiation on a basis mutually advantageous and acceptable for a termination of hostilities and resumption of peaceful relations.

Note: (The foregoing draft of Section III is subject to further discussion of the question of cooperative defense against communistic activities, including the stationing of Japanese troops in Chinese territory, and the question of economic cooperation between China and Japan. With regard to suggestions that the language of Section III be changed, it is believed that consideration of any suggested change can most advantageously be given after all the points in the annex relating to this section have been satisfactorily worked out, when the section and its annex can be viewed as a whole.)

Annex

The basic terms as referred to in the above section are as follows:

a. Neighborly friendship.

b. (Cooperative defense against injurious communistic activities—including the stationing of Japanese troops in Chinese territory.) Subject to further discussion.

c. (Economic cooperation.) Subject to agreement on an exchange of letters in regard to the application to this point of the principle of non-discrimination in international commercial relations.

   d. Mutual respect of sovereignty and territories.

   e. Mutual respect for the inherent characteristics of each nation, cooperating as good neighbors and forming an East Asian nucleus contributing to world peace.

   f. Withdrawal of Japanese armed forces from Chinese territory as promptly as possible and in accordance with an agreement to be concluded between Japan and China.

   g. No annexation.

   h. No indemnities.

   i. Amicable negotiations in regard to Manchoukuo.

Suggested Letter to be Addressed by the Secretary of State to the Japanese Ambassador in Connection with the Joint Declaration

Excellency: In the informal conversations which resulted in the conclusion of a general agreement of understanding between our two Governments, you and your associates expressed fully and frankly views on the intentions of the Japanese Government in regard to applying to Japan's proposed economic cooperation with China the principle of non-discrimination in international commercial relations. It is believed that it would be helpful if you could be so good as to confirm the statements already expressed orally in the form of replies on the following points:

   1. Does the term "economic cooperation" between Japan and China contemplate the granting by the Government of China to the Japanese Government or its nationals of any preferential or monopolistic rights which would discriminate in favor of the Japanese Government and Japanese nationals as compared with the Government and nationals of the United States and of other third countries? Is it contemplated that upon the inauguration of negotiations for a peaceful settlement between Japan and China the special Japanese companies, such as the North China Development Company and the Central China Promotion Company and their subsidiaries, will be divested, in so far as Japanese official support may be involved, of any monopolistic or other preferential rights that they may exercise in fact or that may inure to them by virtue of present circumstances in areas of China under Japanese military occupation?.

   2. With regards to existing restrictions upon freedom of trade and travel by nationals of third countries in Chinese territory under Japanese military occupation, could the Japanese Government indicate approximately what restrictions will be removed immediately upon the entering into by the Government of Chungking of negotiations with the Government of Japan and what restrictions will be removed at later dates, with an indication in each case in so far as possible of the approximate time within which removal of restrictions would be effected?

3. Is it the intention of the Japanese Government that the Chinese Government shall exercise full and complete control of matters relating to trade, currency and exchange? Is it the intention of the Japanese Government to withdraw and to redeem the Japanese military notes which are being circulated in China and the notes of Japanese-sponsored regimes in China? Can the Japanese Government indicate how soon after the inauguration of the contemplated negotiations arrangements to the above ends can in its opinion be carried out?

It would be appreciated if as specific replies as possible could be made to the questions above listed.

Accept, Excellency, the renewed assurances of my highest consideration.

Notes

1. *Foreign Relations: Japan,* II, 398–402.
2. *Ibid.,* II, 420–424.
3. *Ibid.,* II, 446–454.
4. *Ibid.,* II, 473–476.
5. *Ibid.,* II, 486–492.

VI

DETERIORATING CONDITIONS

The American draft of June 21 had hardly been delivered to the Japanese before German armies launched an invasion of the Soviet Union. While this was a part of the European war, the Pacific ramifications were obvious. Japan, participant in a nonaggression pact with Russia, was in an awkward position because of membership in the Axis Alliance. Deeply involved in China, the Japanese had been more concerned about interests to the south than in Siberia. The German attack on Russia renewed the discussion in Tokyo about the direction of Japanese policy.

The invasion of Russia came at a time when those involved in negotiating the draft treaty looked forward to the conclusion of a successful agreement. Father Drought had informed Hull in early July that a new Japanese draft, never formally considered, met all the American objections. But that was not the prevailing feeling about prospects for the treaty among State Department personnel.

Any optimistic feeling about the progress of the draft treaty was muted by a growing hard-line position on trade with Japan. Congress had enacted legislation in May that led to further restrictions on such trade. In June those shipments of American oil that had still been allowed were sharply curtailed by additional restrictions, allegedly imposed because of domestic shortages on the east coast.

Within the Roosevelt Administration, elements led by Treasury Secretary Henry Morgenthau and Assistant Secretary of State Dean Acheson wished to cut off all shipments of oil. Hull, however, feared that a total ban would force the Japanese to more immediate and aggressive action in the East Indies. Until ill health forced him to leave Washington for several weeks in July and August, Hull was able to prevent complete severance of trade in petroleum with Japan.

The swift movement of events during July and August, all a direct result of the the Russo-German War, temporarily brought an end to consideration of a bilateral agreement that might maintain peace in the Pacific.

Japan Outlines Her Policy

Following the outbreak of war between Germany and Russia, three main divisions appeared within the Japanese government regarding a future course of action. Prime Minister Konoye favored a policy of conciliation with the United States, in an attempt to gain by diplomacy what others sought through military conquest. While that would mean that Japan would settle for less than the expansionists sought, it would avoid a break, and possible war, with America.

Foreign Minister Matsuoka, who had negotiated both the Axis Alliance and the Soviet Neutrality Treaty, chose the Axis over the Russians and urged immediate war on Russia in association with Germany. A quick strike against Russia would bring about an end to the fighting before the United States could enter the conflict. Delay might result in an alliance among Britain, Russia and the United States, forcing Japan into isolation or a multifront war.

Military leaders, for the most part, preferred the already agreed upon plan of continuing toward the south. A war with Russia, if not won quickly, would commit Japan to two major conflicts in Asia at a time when resources such as petroleum, obtainable from the south but not from Siberia, had become a critical concern.

The position confirmed at the policy conference on July 2 was the result of several days of debate among those holding the three points of view outlined above. Shortly thereafter Foreign Minister Matsuoka would be forced out of office in a cabinet reshuffle, replaced by Admiral Teijiro Toyoda.

This policy statement and the report of the September 6 council, which follows later in this section, were not among the Japanese documents intercepted and decoded by the American government before the war.

*An Outline of the Policy of the Imperial Government
in View of the Present Developments*[1]

Decision reached at the Conference held in the Imperial Presence on July 2.

I. POLICY

1. The Imperial Government is determined to follow a policy which will result in the establishment of the Greater East Asia Co-prosperity Sphere and world peace, no matter what international developments take place.
2. The Imperial Government will continue its efforts to effect a settlement of the China Incident and seek to establish a solid basis for the security and preservation of the nation. This will involve an advance into the Southern Regions and, depending on future developments, a settlement of the Soviet Question as well.
3. The Imperial Government will carry out the above program no matter what obstacles may be encountered.

II. SUMMARY

1. Steps will be taken to bring pressure on the Chiang Regime from the Southern approaches in order to bring about its surrender. Whenever demanded by future developments the rights of a belligerent will be resorted to against Chungking and hostile concessions taken over.
2. In order to guarantee national security and preservation, the Imperial Government will continue all necessary diplomatic negotiations with reference to the southern regions and also carry out various other plans as may be necessary. In case the diplomatic negotiations break down, preparations for a war with England and America will also be carried forward. First of all, the plans which have been laid with reference to French Indo-China and Thai will be prosecuted, with a view to consolidating our position in the southern territories.

   In carrying out the plans outlined in the foregoing article, we will not be deterred by the possibility of being involved in a war with England and America.
3. Our attitude with reference to the German-Soviet War will be based on the spirit of the Tri-Partite Pact. However, we will not enter the conflict for some time but will steadily proceed with military preparations against the Soviet and decide our final attitude independently. At the same time, we will continue carefully correlated activities in the diplomatic field.

   In case the German-Soviet War should develop to our advantage, we will make use of our military strength, settle the Soviet question and guarantee the safety of our northern borders.

   (Pencilled Note: On this occasion the Army and Foreign Minister Matsuoka took a strong attitude toward the Soviet Union, and the

Army began concentrating its armed forces in Manchoukuo. This resolution was drawn up to offset the policies of the Army and the Foreign Minister.)

4. In carrying out the preceding article all plans, especially the use of armed forces, will be carried out in such a way as to place no serious obstacle in the path of our basic military preparations for a war with England and America.

5. In case all diplomatic means fail to prevent the entrance of America into the European War, we will proceed in harmony with our obligations under the Tri-Partite Pact. However, with reference to the time and method of employing our armed forces we will take independent action.

6. We will immediately turn our attention to placing the nation on a war basis and will take special measures to strengthen the defenses of the nation.

7. Concrete plans covering this program will be drawn up separately.

Roosevelt Warns Japan

Moving to carry out the policy confirmed at the July 2 conference, the Japanese in late July forced the French to allow Japanese armies into southern Indochina. Western reaction was prompt. Roosevelt integrated the armed forces of the Philippines into the American command in the islands, closed the Panama Canal to Japanese shipping, and froze all Japanese assets in the United States, making trade between the two nations virtually impossible. Without technically banning oil sales, the effect was the same. Within two days, both Britain and the Dutch East Indies had cut off the supply of oil and most other goods to Japan.

Though technically Japan was still able to purchase non-aviation grade petroleum, in Hull's absence from the State Department hard-liners who opposed oil sales managed to delay the issuance of export licenses. By the time Hull returned to his desk and realized that a virtual embargo on oil was in effect the ban had been in existence for over a month. He acquiesced, fearing that a resumption of oil sales at that point would only encourage those in Japan who believed the Americans could be coerced into conforming to Japanese policy.

In mid-August British Prime Minister Winston Churchill met with Roosevelt on a warship off Newfoundland. While this conference is best remembered for the "Atlantic Charter" that it produced, it also dealt with Japan. Churchill urged Roosevelt to send a virtual ultimatum to Japan, indicating that, should that nation extend the conflict in Asia to other powers not yet involved, the President would seek a declaration of war from Congress. Watered down by Hull so that the note emphasized the positive efforts by both Japan and the United States to reach an understanding, the warning was delivered to Nomura on August 17.

Oral Statement
Handed by President Roosevelt to the Japanese Ambassador (Nomura)
on August 17, 1941[2]

During past months the Governments of the United States and of Japan, through the Secretary of State and the Japanese Ambassador in Washington, have engaged in protracted conversations directed toward exploring the possibility of reaching a sound basis for negotiations between the two countries relative to the maintenance of peace with order and justice in the Pacific. The principles and policies which were under discussion in these conversations precluded pursuit by either Government of objectives of expansion by force or by threat of force.

On July 24 last the President of the United States informed the Japanese Government through the Japanese Ambassador in Washington that he was willing to suggest to the Governments of Great Britain, of The Netherlands and of China that they make a binding and solemn declaration that they had no aggressive intentions with regard to Indochina and that they would agree that the markets and raw materials of Indochina should be available to all Powers on equal terms. The President stated further that he would be willing to suggest to the Powers mentioned that they undertake this declaration, in which the United States would be willing to join, upon the understanding that the Government of Japan would be disposed to withdraw its military and naval forces from Indochina.

Notwithstanding these efforts, the Government of Japan has continued its military activities and its disposals of armed forces at various points in the Far East and has occupied Indochina with its military, air and naval forces.

The Government of the United States is in full sympathy with the desire expressed by the Japanese Government that there be provided a fresh basis for amicable and mutually profitable relations between our two countries. This Government's patience in seeking an acceptable basis for such an undertaking has been demonstrated time and again during recent years and especially during recent months. This Government feels at the present stage that nothing short of the most complete candor on its part, in the light of evidence and indications which come to it from many sources, will at this moment tend to further the objectives sought.

Such being the case, this Government now finds it necessary to say to the Government of Japan that if the Japanese Government takes any further steps in pursuance of a policy or program of military domination by force or threat of force of neighboring countries, the Government of the United States will be compelled to take immediately any and all steps which it may deem necessary toward safeguarding the legitimate rights and interests of the United States and American nationals and toward insuring the safety and security of the United States.

Japan Plans For War

Faced with the knowledge that their oil reserves and other raw materials would last only a short time, the Japanese military feared that unless diplomatic talks bore fruit soon Japan might be forced to declare war on the western powers without adequate fuel resources. Consequently, Konoye's cabinet met with high ranking military officials in a series of conferences that planned an overall policy to guide Japanese action in the summer and fall of 1941.

At the Imperial Conference on September 6, the Emperor personally intervened to insist that diplomatic rather than military efforts be emphasized as solutions to Japan's problems. But should diplomacy not succeed by early October, the way was cleared for the use of force. The October deadline established at this conference would play a major role in the eventual fall of the Konoye cabinet.

Plans for the Prosecution of the Policy of the Imperial Government[3]

[September 6, 1941]

Agenda for a Council in the Imperial Presence

In view of the increasingly critical situation, especially the aggressive plans being carried out by America, England, Holland and other countries, the situation in Soviet Russia and the Empire's latent potentialities, the Japanese Government will proceed as follows in carrying out its plans for the southern territories as laid in . . . [the July 2 conference].

1. Determined not to be deterred by the possibility of being involved in a war with America (and England and Holland) in order to secure our national existence, we will proceed with war preparations so that they be completed approximately toward the end of October.

2. At the same time, we will endeavor by every possible diplomatic means to have our demands agreed to by America and England. Japan's minimum demands in these negotiations with America (and England), together with the Empire's maximum concessions are embodied in the attached document.

3. If by the early part of October there is no reasonable hope of having our demands agreed to in the diplomatic negotiations mentioned above, we will immediately make up our minds to get ready for war against America (and England and Holland).

Policies with reference to countries other than those in the southern territories will be carried out in harmony with the plans already laid. Special effort will be made to prevent America and Soviet Russia from forming a united front against Japan.

Annex

A list of Japan's minimum demands and her maximum concessions in negotiations with America and England

Japan's Minimum Demands in her Negotiations with America (and England).

1. America and England shall not intervene in or obstruct a settlement by Japan of the China Incident.

    a. They will not interfere with Japan's plan to settle the China Incident in harmony with the Sino-Japanese Basic Agreement and the Japan-China-Manchoukuo Tri Partite Declaration.

    b. America and England will close the Burma Route and offer the Chiang Regime neither military, political nor economic assistance.

        Note: The above do not run counter to Japan's previous declarations in the . . . plan for the settlement of the China Incident. In particular, the plan embodied in the new Sino-Japanese Agreement for the stationing of Japanese troops in the specified areas will be rigidly adhered to. However, the withdrawal of troops other than those mentioned above may be guaranteed in principle upon the settlement of the China Incident.

        Commercial operations in China on the part of America and England may also be guaranteed, in so far as they are purely commercial.

2. America and England will take no action in the Far East which offers a threat to the defense of the Empire.

    a. America and England will not establish military bases in Thai, the Netherlands East Indies, China or Far Eastern Soviet Russia.

    b. Their Far Eastern military forces will not be increased over their present strength.

        Note: Any demands for the liquidation of Japan's special relations with French Indo-China based on the Japanese-French Agreement will not be considered.

3. America and England will cooperate with Japan in her attempt to obtain needed raw materials.
   a. America and England will restore trade relations with Japan and furnish her with the raw materials she needs from the British and American territories in the Southwest Pacific.
   b. America and England will assist Japan to establish close economic relations with Thai and the Netherlands East Indies.

Maximum Concessions by Japan.
It is understood that our minimum demands as listed under I above will be agreed to.

1. Japan will not use French Indo-China as a base for operations against any neighboring countries with the exception of China.

   Note: In case any questions are asked concerning Japan's attitude towards Soviet Russia, the answer is to be that as long as Soviet Russia faithfully carries out the Neutrality Pact and does not violate the spirit of the agreement by, for instance, threatening Japan or Manchuria, Japan will not take any military action.

2. Japan is prepared to withdraw her troops from French Indo-China as soon as a just peace is established in the Far East.

3. Japan is prepared to guarantee the neutrality of the Philippine Islands.

Notes

1. U. S. Congress Joint Committee on the Investigation of the Pearl Harbor Attack, *Pearl Harbor Attack: Hearings Before the Joint Committee . . . 39 parts* (Washington, 1946), part 20, 4018–19.

2. *Foreign Relations: Japan*, II, 556–557.

3. *Pearl Harbor Attack*, part 20, 4022–4023.

VII

THE PACIFIC CONFERENCE

In the late summer of 1941, Japanese moderates initiated their final attempt to reach an accord with the United States and thereby avert a resort to war. Prime Minister Konoye felt that his civilian government could best be strengthened by a meeting between himself and President Roosevelt, and sent such a proposal to the President. Japanese notes, from August into October, frequently stressed the urgency of an American agreement to hold the meeting, and their statements to American diplomats indicated fear that American insistence upon detailed agreements prior to the summit conference would so delay the meeting that a crisis might arise before it could be held.

The American government, with Secretary Hull as its spokesman, demanded certain Japanese commitments as a basis for negotiation, convinced that the proposed meeting would be a "second Munich" without some basic agreement beforehand. Konoye, fearful that the concessions demanded by Hull would topple his already shaky government (he had been forced to reorganize his cabinet in July), insisted that these "details" be left until the conference was held.

In a series of notes in September, the Japanese re-opened the preliminary conversations, which had been suspended by the United States in late June.

Japan Suggests A Solution

Following the Imperial Conference on September 6, Prime Minister Konoye met with Ambassador Grew, assuring the Ambassador that Japan desired a diplomatic solution to existing differences. While Konoye's assurances may have placed a much too optimistic face on the position of the Japanese government, which had just decided for war in the event diplomacy failed (as many in the government expected) it certainly reflected the Prime Minister's desire at that time. Konoye's view was contained in a note designed to reopen the long-suspended treaty negotiations.

Japan to the United States, September 6, 1941[1]

. . . The Government of Japan undertakes:

a. that Japan is ready to express its concurrence in those matters already tentatively agreed upon between Japan and the United States in the course of their preliminary informal conversations;

b. that Japan will not make military advancement from French Indo-China against any of its adjoining areas, and likewise will not, without any justifiable reason, resort to military action against regions lying south of Japan;

c. that the attitudes of Japan and the United States towards the European War will be decided by the concept of protection and self-defense and in case the United States should participate in the European War, the interpretation and execution of the Tripartite Pact by Japan shall be independently decided;

d. that Japan will endeavor to bring about the rehabilitation of general and normal relationships between Japan and China, upon the realization of which Japan is ready to withdraw its armed forces from China in accordance with agreements between Japan and China;

e. that the economic activities of the United States in China will not be restricted so long as pursued on an equitable basis;

f. that Japan's activities in the Southwestern Pacific area will be carried on by peaceful means and in accordance with the principle of non-discrimination in international commerce, and that Japan will cooperate in the production and procurement by the United States of the natural resources of the said area which it needs;

g. that Japan will take measures necessary for the resumption of normal trade relations between Japan and the United States, and in connection with the above mentioned, Japan is ready to discontinue immediately the application of the foreigner's transactions control regulation with regard to the United States on the basis of reciprocity.

The Government of the United States undertakes:

a. that, in response to the Japanese Government's commitment expressed in point (d.) referred to above, the United States will abstain from any measures and actions which will be prejudicial to the endeavor by Japan concerning the settlement of the China Affair;
b. that the United States will reciprocate Japan's commitment expressed in point (f.) referred to above;
c. that the United States will suspend any military measures in the Far East and in the Southwestern Pacific Area:
d. that the United States will immediately (upon settlement) reciprocate Japan's commitment expressed in point (g.) referred to above by discontinuing the application of the so-called freezing act with regard to Japan and further by removing the prohibition against the passage of Japanese vessels through the Panama Canal.

Japan's Peace Terms For China Restated

The main stumbling block to peace in the Pacific had been the China question. This was clearly understood by those on both sides of the Pacific who wished to avoid war. In an effort to resolve differences with the United States over China, a high level conference in Japan on September 13 prepared a final list of Japan's terms for China. To push forward negotiations between Japan and the United States, Konoye delivered to Ambassador Grew on September 22 the newly-developed Japanese terms on which the China affair could be terminated. A comparison with the last American draft, submitted on June 21, indicates substantial movement on the part of Japan. While there was reason for American objection to some of the conditions, Japan had made a major attempt to accomodate concerns previously expressed by the United States.

The Japanese Minister for Foreign Affairs (Toyoda)
to the American Ambassador in Japan (Grew) [2]

[September 22, 1941]

Text of Basic Japanese Terms of Peace with China

1. Neighborly friendship.
2. Respect for sovereignty and territorial integrity.
3. Cooperative defense between Japan and China.
   Cooperation between Japan and China for the purposes of preventing communistic and other subversive activities which may

constitute a menace to the security of both countries and of maintaining public order in China.

Stationing of Japanese troops and naval forces in certain areas in the Chinese territory for a necessary period for the purposes referred to above and in accordance with the existing agreements and usages.

4. Withdrawal of Japanese armed forces.

The Japanese armed forces which have been dispatched to China for carrying out the China Affairs will be withdrawn from China upon the settlement of the said Affairs, excepting those troops which come under point 3.

5. Economic cooperation.
   a. There shall be economic cooperation between Japan and China, having the development and utilization of essential materials for national defense in China as its principal objective.
   b. The preceding paragraph does not mean to restrict any economic activities by third Powers in China so long as they are pursued on an equitable basis.

6. Fusion of the Chiang Kai-shek regime and the Wang Ching-wei Government.

7. No annexation.

8. No indemnities.

9. Recognition of Manchoukuo.

Japan's Last Formal Draft

A few days after presentation of Japan's terms for peace in China, Grew received from the foreign office the last revision of the draft treaty that had been under consideration since early April. Recognizing that Japan's advance into southern Indochina had precipitated increased restrictions on her foreign trade, the new draft made specific reference to Japanese willingness to withdraw from Indochina upon termination of the war in China. The revised draft contained only general statements regarding China, but that subject had been covered in much more detail in the September 22 note.

From the standpoint of Konoye, there was a great deal of urgency about this final draft. Under increasing pressure at home to end diplomatic discussions and to unleash the military, he recognized that the draft, coupled with his plea to Hull for a face-to-face meeting with Roosevelt, represented the last chance to prevent war.

With the October deadline only a few days away, Konoye pleaded with Grew to impress upon Hull the necessity of the summit.

Toyoda to Grew, September 25, 1941[3]

... Both Governments presume to anticipate that they could achieve harmonious relations if certain situations and attitudes were clarified or improved, to wit:

1. The concepts of Japan and of the United States respecting international relations and the character of nations.
2. The attitudes of both Governments toward the European War.
3. Action toward a peaceful settlement between Japan and China.
4. Commerce between both nations.
5. Economic problems in the Southwestern Pacific area.
6. The policies of both nations affecting political stabilization in the Pacific area.

Accordingly, the Government of Japan and the Government of the United States have come to the following mutual understanding and declaration of policy: ...

2. *The attitudes of both Governments toward the European War.*

Both Governments maintain it their common aim to bring about peace in the world, and, when an opportune time arrives, they will endeavor jointly for the early restoration of world peace.

With regard to developments of the situation prior to the restoration of world peace, both Governments will be guided in their conduct by considerations of protection and self-defense; and, in case the United States should participate in the European War, Japan would decide entirely independently in the matter of interpretation of the Tripartite pact between Japan, Germany and Italy, and would likewise determine what actions might be taken by way of fulfilling the obligations in accordance with the said interpretation.

3. *Action toward a peaceful settlement between Japan and China.*

Both Governments, taking cognizance of the fact that the settlement of the China Affair has a vital bearing upon the peace of the entire Pacific area and consequently upon that of the world, will endeavor to expedite a rapid realization of the settlement of the said Affair.

The Government of the United States, recognizing the effort and the sincere desire on the part of the Japanese Government concerning the peaceful settlement of the China Affair, will, with the intention of facilitating the realization of the settlement, render its good offices in order that the Chungking Government may promptly enter into negotiations with the Government of Japan for a termination of hostilities and a resumption of peaceful relations, and will refrain from resorting to any measures and actions which might hamper the measures and efforts of the Government of Japan directed toward the settlement of the China Affair.

The Government of Japan maintains that the basic general terms of peace for the settlement of the China Affair will be in harmony with the principles embodied in the Konoye statement, and those agreements between Japan and China and those matters which have been put into effect in accordance with the said statement; that the economic cooperation between Japan and China will be carried on by peaceful means and in conformity with the principle of non-discrimination in the international commercial relations and also with the principle of especially close relationship which is natural between neighboring countries; and that the economic activities of third Powers in China will not be excluded so long as they are pursued on an equitable basis. . . .

4. *Commerce between Japan and the United States.*

Both Governments agree to take without delay measures necessary for resuming normal trade relations between the two countries.

Both Governments guarantee each other that they will, as the first of the measures envisaged in the preceding paragraph, discontinue immediately the measures of freezing assets now being enforced, and that they will supply mutually such commodities as are, respectively, available and required by either of them.

5. *Economic problems in the Southwestern Pacific area.*

Both Governments mutually pledge themselves that the economic activities of Japan and the United States in the Southwestern Pacific area shall be carried on by peaceful means and in conformity with the principle of non-discrimination in the international commercial relations in pursuance of the policy stated in the preceding paragraph, both Governments agree to cooperate each with the other towards the creation of conditions in international trade and international investment under which both countries will have a reasonable opportunity to secure through the trade process the means of acquiring those goods and commodities which each country needs for the safeguarding and development of its own economy.

Both Governments will amicably cooperate for the conclusion and execution of agreements with the Powers concerned in regard to the production and supply, on the basis of non-discrimination, of such specific commodities as oil, rubber, nickel, and tin.

6. *The policies of both nations affecting political stabilization in the Pacific area.*

Both Governments, taking cognizance of the fact that it is a matter of vital importance to stabilize promptly the situation in the Southwestern Pacific area, undertake not to resort to any measures and actions which may jeopardize such stabilization. The Government of Japan will not make any armed advancement, using French Indo-China as a base, to any adjacent area thereof (excluding China), and, upon the establishment of an equitable peace in the Pacific area, will withdraw its troops which are now stationed in French Indo-China.

The Government of the United States will alleviate its military measures in the Southwestern Pacific area.

Both Governments declare that they respect the sovereignty and territorial integrity of Thailand and Netherland East Indies, and that they are prepared to conclude an agreement concerning the neutralization of the Philippine Islands when its independence will have been achieved.

The Government of the United States guarantees non-discriminatory treatment of the Japanese nationals in the Philippine Islands.

Grew Urges Acceptance

Ambassador Grew did not have to be convinced by Konoye of the importance of a summit meeting between the two heads of state. Fully aware of the precarious relationship then existing between the United States and Japan, and fearful that the fall of Konoye would find the pendulum swinging toward the militarists, Grew repeatedly urged Hull and Roosevelt to work with Konoye. Though he had been less than enthusiastic in his assessment of Konoye in the letter to Roosevelt in December, 1940, by September Grew saw the survival of Konoye's cabinet as the last hope for a peaceful settlement. Hardly a liberal, Konoye nevertheless represented the moderate tradition that relied on diplomacy and civil authority rather than a military solution.

Foreign Minister Toyoda, mindful of the timetable established by the September 6 Imperial Conference, urged that the Roosevelt-Konoye meeting be held prior to October 15. On September 29 Grew, with his customary deference and uncanny understanding of Japanese politics, cabled this advice to Hull.

Grew to Hull, September 29, 1941[4]

The Ambassador reports for Secretary Hull and Under Secretary Welles as follows:

1. In regard to the preliminary conversations taking place at Washington and Tokyo, the Ambassador points out that a review of telegraphic correspondence on this subject since last spring reveals the Japanese Government's efforts, increasing steadily and intensified lately, to arrange a meeting between Prince Konoye and President Roosevelt without further delay. While admitting his role to be chiefly

that of a transmitting agent in these conversations, the Ambassador naturally wishes to aid in any constructive way, particularly by endeavoring to appraise accurately for the President and the Secretary of State the Japanese factors and conditions having direct or indirect bearing on the subject and also by trying to bring the Japanese Government to adopt measures and policies such as the United States Government deems to be essential for a mutual understanding or agreement between Japan and the United states. . . . The Ambassador expresses his earnest hope therefore that so propitious a period be not permitted to slip by without a new foundation having been laid with enough stability to warrant a reasonable amount of confidence that the structure to be erected gradually and progressively thereupon can and will endure.

2. [Grew reiterated the main points of his December 14, 1940, analysis of Japanese-American relations.]

3. The Ambassador suggests that the United States has been following very wisely precisely this policy which, furthered by other developments in the world, has helped to discredit Japanese leadership, notably that of former Foreign Minister Matsuoka. The Ambassador cites as world developments arousing a positive reaction from the United States the conclusion by Japan of the Tripartite Alliance and Japan's recognition of the Wang Ching-wei regime at Nanking, which preceded Germany's attack on the Soviet Union. Germany's action upset the basis for the Tripartite Pact, Japan having joined the Italo-German Axis in order to obtain security against Russia and thereby to avoid the peril of being caught between the Soviet Union and the United States. At the present time Japan is attempting to correct this miscalculation by getting out of an extremely dangerous position. The Ambassador recalls his reports to the Department to the effect that Japanese foreign policies are inevitably changed by the impact of events abroad and that liberal elements in Japan might come to the top in due course as a result of the trend of events. He considers that such a time has arrived. He sees a good chance of Japan's falling into line if a program can be followed of world reconstruction as forecast by the Declaration of President Roosevelt and Prime Minister Churchill. American policy—of forebearance, patient argumentation, efforts at persuasion, followed for many years, plus a manifest determination of the United States to take positive measures when called for—plus the impact of world developments upon Japan, has rendered Japan's political soil hospitable to the sowing of new seeds which, the Ambassador feels, if planted carefully and nourished, may bring about the anticipated regeneration of Japanese thought and a complete readjustment of relations between Japan and the United States.

4. Certain quarters have advanced the thought—and no doubt it is prominently in the mind of the United States Government—that at this juncture an agreement between Japan and the United States will serve merely as a breathing spell to Japan. During such a breathing spell, Japan, having successfully untangled itself with American aid from the China conflict, will recoup and strengthen its forces in order to resume at the next favorable opportunity its expansionist program. This thought cannot be gainsaid with certainty. . . . The Ambassador adds that should this thesis be accepted as reasonably sound, the position will confront the United States of choosing one of two methods to approach its objective, namely, either the method of progressive economic strangulation or the method of constructive conciliation, not so-called appeasement. The Ambassador sees the second method as the definite choice of the United States Government following the beginning of the Washington preliminary conversations and President Roosevelt's acceptance in principle of the Japanese Prime Minister's proposed meeting. . . .

5. The Ambassador, while admitting that risks will inevitably be involved no matter what course is pursued toward Japan, offers his carefully studied belief that there would be substantial hope at the very least of preventing the Far Eastern situation from becoming worse and perhaps of ensuring definitely constructive results, if an agreement along the lines of the preliminary discussions were brought to a head by the proposed meeting of the heads of the two Governments. . . .

6. Certain quarters hold the view that it is altogether improbable under existing circumstances that counteraction will be deliberately taken by Japan in response to any American action likely to be taken in the Pacific which would bring about war with the United States. The Ambassador states his inability to agree that war may not supervene following actions, whether irrational or deliberate, by elements either in Japan or in the United States tending so to inflame public opinion in the other country concerned as to make war unavoidable. He recalls in this regard the cases of the *Maine* and the *Panay*.

7. The Ambassador stresses the importance of understanding Japanese psychology, fundamentally unlike that of any Western nation. . . .

8. Should the United States expect or await agreement by the Japanese Government, in the present preliminary conversations, to clear-cut commitments which will satisfy the United States Government both as to principle and as to concrete detail, almost certainly the conversations will drag along indefinitely and unproductively until the Konoye Cabinet and its supporting elements desiring *rapprochement* with the United States will come to the conclusion that the outlook for an agreement is hopeless and that the United States Government is only playing for time. . . .

9. The Ambassador continues by stating that he has been emphatically told on numerous occasions—and such declarations he considers must be accepted at their face value—that prior to the proposed Roosevelt-Konoye meeting and formal negotiations it is impossible for the Japanese Government to define its future assurances and commitments more specifically than hitherto stated. . . . Although certain basic principles have been accepted provisionally by the Japanese Government, the definitions and formulae of Japan's future objectives and policy as advanced so far during the preliminary conversations, and the statements supplementary to those definitions, are so abstract or equivocal and are open to such wide interpretation that they rather create confusion than clarify commitments which the Japanese government is ready to undertake. . . . The Ambassador therefore does not consider unlikely the possibility of Prince Konoye's being in a position to give President Roosevelt directly a more explicit and satisfactory engagement than has already been vouchsafed in the course of the preliminary conversations.

10. In the opinion of the Ambassador, on the basis of the above observations which he has every reason to regard as sound, American objectives will not be reached by insisting or continuing to insist during the preliminary conversations that Japan provide the sort of clear-cut, specific commitments which appear in any final, formal convention or treaty. Unless a reasonable amount of confidence is placed by the United States in the professed sincerity of intention and good faith of Prince Konoye and his supporters to mould Japan's future policy upon the basic principles they are ready to accept and then to adopt those measures which gradually but loyally implement those principles, with it understood that the United States will implement its own commitments *pari passu* with the steps which Japan takes, the Ambassador does not believe that a new orientation can be successfully created in Japan to lead to a general improving of Japanese-American relations and to the hope that ultimate war may be avoided in the Pacific. The sole way to discredit the Japanese military machine and army is through wholesale military defeat, and the Ambassador sees no present prospect of this. The only alternative (and the only wise one in the view of the Ambassador) is an attempt to produce a regeneration of Japanese thought and outlook through constructive conciliation, along the lines of American efforts at present. The Ambassador inquires whether the better part of wisdom and of statesmanship is not to bring such efforts to a head before the force of their initial impetus is lost, leaving it impossible to overcome an opposition which the Ambassador thinks will mount inevitably and steadily in Japan. . . .

Hull Rejects The Conference Proposal

By early October Hull had abandoned the moderate position he had maintained earlier in the year when he had struggled with Acheson, Hornbeck, and Morgenthau to prevent a hard-line position that might have forced Japan into war. Now he was convinced that Konoye and other Japanese moderates could not control the military and that the time for a diplomatic settlement had passed. On October 2 Hull met with Nomura and ruled out any conference. The note Hull presented to Nomura made clear that the United States no longer was willing to concede to Japan special rights based on her geographic location. His formal rejection in this October 2 note of Japan's September 25th draft and of the conference idea assured the fall of the Konoye government and the unchallenged ascendancy of Japanese expansionists.

Hull to Nomura, October 2, 1941[5]

. . . The Government of the United States welcomed, as affording a possible opportunity for furthering the broad-gauge objectives and principles of a program of peace, the Japanese Government's suggestion made through its Ambassador here in the early part of August that there be held a meeting of the responsible heads of the Japanese Government and of the Government of the United States to discuss means for bringing about an adjustment of relations between the United States and Japan and that there be resumed the informal conversations which had been in progress between the two countries to ascertain whether there existed a basis for negotiations relative to a peaceful settlement covering the entire Pacific situation. . . .

In the light of the broad purposes and fundamental principles which this Government holds, it was gratifying to the President and the Government of the United States to receive the message of the Prime Minister and the statement of the Government of Japan on August 28, 1941, containing statements expressing Japan's desire and intent to pursue courses of peace in harmony with the fundamental principles to which the people and Government of the United States are committed. . . .

The Government of the United States, while desiring to proceed as rapidly as possible with consideration of arrangements for a meeting between the heads of state, felt it desirable, in order to assure that the meeting would accomplish the objectives in view, to clarify the interpretation of certain principles and the practical application thereof to concrete problems in the Pacific area. It has not been the purpose of this Government to enter into a discussion of details; this Government has felt, however, that the clarification sought would afford a means of expediting our effort to arrive at a meeting of minds.

On September 3, 1941, the President . . . reiterated the four principles regarded by this Government as the foundation upon which relations between nations should properly rest. Those principles are:

1. Respect for the territorial integrity and the sovereignty of each and all nations.
2. Support of the principle of non-interference in the internal affairs of other countries.
3. Support of the principle of equality, including equality of commercial opportunity.
4. Non-disturbance of the *status quo* in the Pacific except as the *status quo* may be altered by peaceful means.

On September 6, the Prime Minister of Japan in a conversation with the American Ambassador at Tokyo stated that he subscribed fully to the four principles above mentioned.

The foregoing developments and assurances, together with other statements made by the Japanese Government, seemed to justify this Government in concluding that the Japanese Government might be expected to adhere to and to give practical application to a broad progressive program covering the entire Pacific area. It was therefore a source of disappointment to the Government of the United States that the proposals of the Japanese Government presented by the Japanese Ambassador on September 6, 1941, which the Japanese Government apparently intended should constitute a concrete basis for discussions, appeared to disclose divergence in the concepts of the two Governments. That is to say, those proposals and the subsequent explanatory statements made in regard thereto serve, in the opinion of this Government, to narrow and restrict not only the application of the principles upon which our informal conversations already referred to had been based but also the various assurances given by the Japanese Government of its desire to move along with the United States in putting into operation a broad program looking to the establishment and maintenance of peace and stability in the entire Pacific area.

As has already been said, the various broad assurances given by the Japanese Premier and the Japanese Government are highly gratifying. In putting forward its attitude of peaceful intent toward other nations, the Japanese Government qualified its assurances with certain phrases the need for which is not easily understood. It is difficult to conceive of there developing under present circumstances in any of the territories neighboring French Indochina, in Thailand or in the Soviet Union any aggressive threat or provocation to Japan. The inalienable right of self-defense is of course well recognized by all nations and there could arise in some minds a question as to just what the Japanese Government has in view in circumscribing its assurances of peaceful intent with what would seem to be unnecessary qualifying phrases.

In the informal conversations there was tentatively arrived at a formula in regard to economic policy . . . which provided that Japanese activity and American activity in the Pacific area shall be carried on by peaceful means and in conformity with the principle of non-discrimination in international commercial relations. In the Japanese Government's proposals of September 6 and in subsequent communications from the Japanese Government the commitments contained in that formula were restricted to the countries of the Southwest Pacific areas (not the Pacific area as a whole). In reference to China the Japanese Government states that it will respect the principle of non-discrimination, but the explanation given in regard to this point would seem to be open to the implication that the Japanese Government has in mind some limitation upon the application of this principle occasioned by reasons of Japan's geographical propinquity to China.

Obviously, it would not be likely to serve the purposes affirmed by the Japanese Government or by this Government if either the United States or Japan were to pursue one course or policy in certain areas while at the same time pursuing an opposite course or policy in other areas.

This Government has noted the views of the Japanese Government in support of its desire to station troops for an indeterminate period in certain areas of China. Entirely apart from the question of the reasons for such a proposal, the inclusion of such a provision in the proposed terms of a peaceful settlement between Japan and China at a time when Japan is in military occupation of large areas in China is open to certain objections. For example, when a country in military occupation of territory of another country proposes to the second country the continued stationing of troops of the first country in certain areas as a condition for a peaceful settlement and thus for the withdrawal of the occupationary forces from other areas, such procedure would seem to be out of keeping with the progessive and enlightened courses and principles which were discussed in the informal conversations and thus would not, in the opinion of this Government, make for peace or offer prospects of stability.

It is believed that a clear-cut manifestation of Japan's intention in regard to the withdrawal of Japanese troops from China and French Indochina would be most helpful in making known—in particular to those who might be inclined to be critical—Japan's peaceful intentions and Japan's desire to follow courses calculated to establish a sound basis for future stability and progress in the Pacific area.

With reference to the attitude of each country toward the European war, this Government has noted with appreciation the further step taken by the Japanese Government to meet the difficulties inherent in this aspect of the relations between the two countries. It is believed that it would be helpful if the Japanese Government could give further study to the question of possible additional clarification of its position.

In the exchanges of views which have taken place between the two Governments in an effort to reach an agreement in principle upon the fundamental questions in order to prepare the ground for the proposed meeting of the responsible chiefs of government, this Government has endeavored to make clear that what it envisages is a comprehensive program calling for the application uniformly to the entire Pacific area of liberal and progressive principles. From what the Japanese Government has so far indicated in regard to its purposes this Government derives the impression that the Japanese Government has in mind a program which would be circumscribed by the imposition of qualifications and exceptions to the actual application of those principles.

If this impression is correct, can the Japanese Government feel that a meeting between the responsible heads of government under such circumstances would be likely to contribute to the advancement of the high purposes which we mutually had in mind?

. . . The subject of the meeting proposed by the Prime Minister and the objectives sought have engaged, and continue to engage, the close and active interest of the President of the United States, and it is the President's earnest hope that discussion of the fundamental questions may be so developed that such a meeting can be held. It is also the President's hope that the Japanese Government shares the convictions of this Government that if the Governments of Japan and the United States are resolved to give those principles practical and comprehensive application, the two Governments can work out a fundamental rehabilitation of the relations between the United States and Japan and contribute to the bringing about of a lasting peace with justice, equity and order in the whole Pacific area.

Notes

1. *Foreign Relations: Japan,* II, 608–609.
2. *Ibid.,* II, 633.
3. *Ibid.,* II, 637–640.
4. *Ibid.,* II, 645–650.
5. *Ibid.,* II, 656–661.

VIII

A LAST DIPLOMATIC EFFORT

Following Hull's rejection of both the conference and Japan's final draft, the top echelon of Japan's government was forced to hold extremely serious discussions regarding that nation's course of action. For several days in mid-October cabinet members met to debate continued negotiations or a direct recourse to war. General Hideki Tojo, Konoye's War Minister, who had led the opposition in the cabinet to continued negotiations, now spoke out even more vigorously for reliance on a military solution. Nothing short of complete withdrawal from China seemed to satisfy the Americans, he noted, and that was unacceptable.

Konoye and Foreign Minister Toyoda suggested that compromise on the question of withdrawal was not out of the question. Such withdrawal might only be temporary or involve a partial troop removal, but, if it satisfied the Americans, war might still be avoided. The navy was reluctant to go to war if other options were available, but Tojo refused to accept any proposal for withdrawal, regardless of its nature. To back down in order to appease the Americans would be harmful to Japanese interests not only in China but elsewhere as well.

In the face of overwhelming opposition to his desire to seek a compromise with the United States, Konoye submitted his resignation and his cabinet fell on October 16. Selected as his successor was the outspoken War Minister, Tojo.

The government of General Tojo showed a greater willingness to continue discussions than most observers expected. In part this was due to the Emperor's personal call for further negotiations with the United States. It was also due to the navy's hesitancy to engage the United States in war at that time. So, despite the September 6 decision to move toward war if negotiations had not been successful by early October and, despite the fact that Konoye had fallen because of his reliance on diplomacy and compromise, Tojo turned to yet another round of discussions. In the meantime, Japanese military units positioned themselves for an attack upon the United States when, as they expected, the negotiations finally broke down.

The Stark-Marshall Memorandum

While the American military had well-detailed plans in the event of war with Japan, the fact remained that a military defense of the Philippine Islands and the Open Door were still beyond the ability of American armed forces. This had been recognized since the presidency of Theodore Roosevelt, though a less compromising policy since 1931 had somewhat obscured it. Now, with the United States at the brink of war with Japan, the nation belatedly moved to build up its forces in the Western Pacific.

Unlike their counterparts in the Japanese army, who clamored for war rather than diplomacy, American commanders sought more time. That view was shared by the two top ranking American military commanders: General George Marshall, Army Chief of Staff, and Admiral Harold Stark, Chief of Naval Operations. The two jointly authored a memorandum to President Roosevelt in early November that raised serious doubts about the wisdom of immediate military operations against Japan.

Memorandum for President Roosevelt[1]

[November 5, 1941]

The Chief of Naval Operations and the Chief of Staff have reexamined the military situation in the Far East. . . . Despatches have indicated it to be Chiang Kai-Shek's belief that a Japanese attack on Kunming is imminent, and the military support from outside sources, particularly by the use of United States and British air units, is the sole hope for defeat of this threat. The Secretary of State has requested advice as to the attitude which this Government should take toward a Japanese offensive against Kunming and the Burma Road.

There is little doubt that a Japanese offensive against the Burma Road would be a very severe blow to the Chinese Central Government. The result might even be the collapse of further effective military resistance by that Government, and thus the liquidation by Japan of the "China Incident." If use of the Burma Road is lost, United States and British Commonwealth aid to China will be seriously curtailed for some months. If resistance by the Chinese Central Government ceases, the need for Japanese troops in China will be reduced. These troops can then be employed elsewhere, after the lapse of time sufficient to permit their withdrawal.

Concentration of Japanese troops for the contemplated offensive, based in northern Indo-China, cannot be completed in less than about two months, although initial offensive operations might be undertaken before that time. The advance towards Kunming over nearly three hundred miles of rough country, with poor communications, will be extremely difficult. The maintenance of supply lines will not be easy. The Chinese, on favorable defense terrain, would have a good chance of defeating this offensive by the use of ground troops alone, provided those troops are adequate in quality and numbers.

The question that the Chief of Naval Operations and the Chief of Staff have taken under consideration is whether or not the United States is justified in undertaking offensive military operations with U. S. forces against Japan, to prevent her from severing the Burma Road. They consider that such operations, however well disguised, would lead to war.

At the present time the United States Fleet in the Pacific is inferior to the Japanese Fleet, and cannot undertake an unlimited offensive in the Western Pacific. In order to be able to do so, it would have to be strengthened by withdrawing [handwritten insertion: "practically"] all naval vessels from the Atlantic except those assigned to local defense forces. An unlimited offensive by the Pacific Fleet would require tremendous merchant tonnage, which could only be withdrawn from services now considered essential. The result of withdrawals from the Atlantic of naval and merchant strength might well cause the United Kingdom to lose the Battle of the Atlantic in the near future.

The only existing [handwritten "current" substituted, "only existing" lined out] plans for war against Japan in the Far East are to conduct defensive war, in cooperation with the British and Dutch, for the defense of the Philippines and the British and Dutch Indies. The Philippines are now being reinforced. The present combined naval, air, and ground forces will make attack on the islands a hazardous undertaking. By about the middle of December, 1941, United States air and submarine strength in the Philippines will have become a positive threat to any Japanese operations south of Formosa. The U. S. Army air forces in the Philippines will have reached the projected strength by February or March, 1942. The potency of this threat will have then increased to a point where it might well be a deciding factor in deterring Japan in operations in the area south and west of the Philippines. By this time, additional British naval and air reinforcements to Singapore will have arrived. The general defensive strength of the entire southern area against possible Japanese operations will have reached impressive proportions.

Until such time as the Burma Road is closed, aid can be extended to Chiang Kai-Shek by measures which probably will not result in war with Japan. These measures are: continuation of economic pressure against Japan, supplying increasing amounts of munitions under the Lend-Lease, and continuation and acceleration of aid to the American Volunteer Group.

The Chief of Naval Operations and the Chief of Staff are in accord in the following conclusions:

a. The basic military policies and strategy agreed to in the United States-British Staff conversations remain sound. The primary objective of the two nations is the defeat of Germany. If Japan be defeated and Germany remain undefeated, decision will still not have been reached. In any case, an unlimited offensive war should not be undertaken against Japan, since such a war would greatly weaken the combined effort in the Atlantic against Germany, the most dangerous enemy.

b. War between the United States and Japan should be avoided while building up the defensive forces in the Far East, until such time as Japan attacks or directly threatens territories whose security to the United States is of very great importance. Military action against Japan should be undertaken only in one or more of the following contingencies:

   1. A direct act of war by Japanese armed forces against the territory or mandated territory of the United States, the British Commonwealth, or the Netherlands East Indies.

   2. The movement of Japanese forces into Thailand (Siam) to the west of 100° East or south of 10° North; or into Portuguese Timor, New Caledonia, or the Loyalty Islands.

c. If the war with Japan cannot be avoided, it should follow the strategic lines of existing war plans; i. e., military operations should be primarily defensive, with the object of holding territory, and weakening Japan's economic position.

d. Considering world strategy, a Japanese advance against Kunming, into Thailand except as previously indicated, or an attack on Russia, would not justify intervention by the United States against Japan.

e. All possible aid short of actual war against Japan should be extended to the Chinese Central Government.

f. In case it is decided to undertake war against Japan, complete coordinated action in the diplomatic, economic, and military fields should be undertaken in common by the United States, the British Commonwealth, and the Netherlands East Indies.

The Chief of Naval Operations and the Chief of Staff recommend that the United States policy in the Far East be based on the above recommendations.

Specifically they recommend:

That the dispatch of United States armed forces for intervention against Japan in China be disapproved.

That material aid to China be accelerated consonant with the needs of Russia, Great Britain and our own armed forces.

That aid to the American Volunteer Group be continued and accelerated to the maximum practicable extent.

That no ultimatum be delivered to Japan.

Japan's Propospal A

Tojo's diplomatic effort consisted primarily of two proposals. Proposal A, to be presented first, was to be used as a basis for bargaining. Proposal B, a *modus vivendi*, was to be the final Japanese diplomatic effort, to be delivered upon American rejection of Proposal A. If the United States did not respond favorably by November 15, Japan would go to war. The deadline was dictated by considerations of weather, which made December the latest possible month for military action before the monsoon season occurred, and by Japan's dwindling supply of oil.

Underlining the seriousness of the diplomatic crisis was Japan's decision to send a special envoy, Saburo Kurusu, to Washington to assist Nomura in the negotiations. He arrived in mid-November, in time to participate in the last-ditch efforts to gain American acceptance of Japan's final offer.

Proposal A[2]

(Secret)

From: Tokyo
To: [Japanese Embassy in] Washington
November 4, 1941

This proposal* is our revised ultimatum made as a result of our attempts to meet, insofar as possible, the wishes of the Americans, clarified

---

* The formal version of Proposal A, delivered to the U. S. on November 7, was based on this note.

as a result of negotiations based on our proposals of September 25. We have toned down our insistences as follows:

1. The question of non-discrimination in trade.

Should they appear not to accede to our proposal of September 25 in this respect, insert the following statement, "The Japanese Government is prepared to carry out this principle in the entire Pacific area; that is to say, China as well, providing the principles of non-discrimination are applied to the entire world."

2. The question of our understanding and application of the Tripartite Alliance.

At the same time that you clarify to them that we intend no expansion of our sphere of self-defense, make clear, as has been repeatedly explained in the past, that we desire to avoid the expansion of Europe's war into the Pacific.

3. The question concerning the evacuation of troops.

We are toning down our stipulations in this connection as follows:

a. The stationing and evacuation of troops in China since the outbreak of the China incident.

Japanese troops which have been sent to China will be stationed in North China, on the Mongolian border regions, and on the island of Hainan, after the establishment of peace between Japan and China, and will not be evacuated until the elapse of a "suitable interval." The evacuation of other troops will be carried out by Japan and China at the same time that peace is established. In order to maintain peace and order, this will be carried out within a period of two years. (Note: Should the American authorities question you in regard to "the suitable period," answer vaguely that such a period should encompass 25 years.)

b. The stationing and evacuation of troops in French Indo-China.

The Japanese Government respects the territorial integrity of the French possession, Indo-China. In the event that a just peace is established, or that the China Incident is brought to a successful conclusion, Japanese troops which have been dispatched to French Indo-China and are there now shall be evacuated.

As a matter of principle we are anxious to avoid having this inserted in the draft of the formal proposal reached between Japan and the United States (whether it is called an understanding proposal or some other sort of a statement.)

Explanation

1. Of course, there is the question of geographical proximity when we come to consider non-discrimination in commerce. However, we have revised our demands along this line hitherto and put the question of non-discrimination on a world-wide basis. In a memorandum of the

American Government, they state in effect, however, that it might be feasible for either country within a certain specified area to adopt a given policy and for the other party within another specified area to adopt a complementary policy. Judging from this statement, I do not believe they will oppose this term. I think that we can easily reach an understanding on this matter.

2. As for the question of the Three-Power Pact, your various messages lead me to believe that the United States is, in general, satisfied with our proposals, so if we make our position even more clear by saying that we will not randomly enlarge upon our interpretation of the right of self-defense, I feel sure that we will soon be mutually agreed on this point.

3. I think that in all probability the question of evacuation will be the hardest. However, in view of the fact that the United States is so much opposed to our stationing soldiers in undefined areas, our purpose is to shift the regions of occupations and our officials, thus attempting to dispel their suspicions. We will call it evacuation; but although it would please the United States for us to make occupation the exception rather than the rule, in the last analysis this would be out of the question. Furthermore, on the matter of duration of occupation, whenever pressed to give a clear statement we have hitherto couched our answers in vague terms. I want you in as indecisive yet as pleasant language as possible to euphemize and try to impart to them the effect that unlimited occupation does not mean perpetual occupation. Summing this up, Proposal A accepts completely America's demands on two of the three proposals mentioned in the other proposal, but when it comes to the last point concerning stationing and evacuation of forces, we have already made our last possible concession. How hard, indeed, have we fought in China for four years! What tremendous sacrifices have we made! They must know this, so their demands in this connection must have been only "wishful thinking." In any case, our internal situation also makes it impossible for us to make any further compromise in this connection. As best you can, please endeavor to have the United States understand this, and I earnestly hope and pray that you can quickly bring about an understanding.

The Abortive *Modus Vivendi*

American military intelligence had broken the Japanese diplomatic code so that civilian and military leaders in Washington were aware of foreign office dispatches to Nomura as soon as he was.

Twenty years earlier American diplomats at the Washington Conference had gained an enormous bargaining advantage when similar code-breaking efforts had told them just how far the Japanese were prepared to go in naval disarmament. Now Hull and Roosevelt were aware of Japanese intentions regarding Proposals A and B.

Proposal A, which had been intercepted before its formal delivery on November 7, was rejected very quickly by Roosevelt, who asked for positive signs from Japan of that nation's intent to pursue a peaceful course. On November 20 Ambassador Nomura submitted Proposal B to Secretary Hull. Through other Japanese messages that had been intercepted by American intelligence, the United States knew that this was Japan's final offer and that the deadline, now extended to November 29, was firm.

Roosevelt was taken with the plan for a *modus vivendi*, for the idea of buying time with a temporary arrangement could be supported on several grounds. He had just been warned by Stark and Marshall that American forces in the Far East would not be fully prepared for war until early 1942, and a few more months would be to America's advantage. In addition, if the Japanese resort to force could be delayed long enough, Japan would have to postpone any military engagement until the weather had improved, giving the United States additional time, and would face the prospect of running out of oil by the delay sanctioned by the *modus vivendi*. Time, which a *modus vivendi* provided, seemed to be on the side of the United States.

Several drafts of a possible American response circulated in Washington even before Proposal B had been formally presented to Hull. All of them were conciliatory and offered the possibility of further negotiation with Japan. Joseph Ballantine, a Far East expert in State, and Harry White, in Treasury, developed separate but equally conciliatory plans.

By late November Secretary Hull had on his desk a counteroffer that, had it been sent, would have been the basis for continued discussion. Given the division within the Japanese government, which had already forced postponement of the "end of negotiations" deadline, receipt in Tokyo of a reasonable alternative to Proposal B might have been to America's advantage, either in delaying war or preventing it.

Japan's Proposal B

Draft Proposal [3]
Handed by the Japanese Ambassador (Nomura)
to the Secretary of State, November 20, 1941

1. Both the Governments of Japan and the United States undertake not to make any armed advancement into any of the regions in the South-eastern Asia and the Southern Pacific area excepting the part of French Indo-China where the Japanese troops are stationed at present.
2. The Japanese Government undertakes to withdraw its troops now stationed in French Indo-China upon either the restoration of peace between Japan and China or the establishment of an equitable peace in the Pacific area.

    In the meantime the Government of Japan declares that it is prepared to remove its troops now stationed in the southern part of French Indo-China to the northern part of the said territory upon the conclusion of the present arrangement, which shall later be embodied in the final agreement.
3. The Governments of Japan and the United States shall cooperate with a view to securing the acquisition of those goods and commodities which the two countries need in Netherlands East Indies.
4. The Governments of Japan and the United States mutually undertake to restore their commercial relations to those prevailing prior to the freezing of the assets.

    The Government of the United States shall supply Japan a required quantity of oil.
5. The Government of the United States undertakes to refrain from such measures and actions as will be prejudicial to the endeavors for the restoration of general peace between Japan and China.

Hull's Undelivered *Modus Vivendi*[4]

1. The Government of the United States and the Government of Japan, both being solicitous for the peace of the Pacific, affirm that their national policies are directed toward lasting and extensive peace throughout the Pacific area and they have no territorial designs therein. They undertake reciprocally not to make by force or threat of force, unless they are attacked, any advancement, from points at which they have military establishments, across any international border in the Pacific area.
2. The Japanese Government undertakes forthwith to withdraw its armed forces now stationed in southern French Indochina, not to engage in any further military activities there, including the construction

of military facilities, and to limit Japanese military forces in northern French Indochina to the number there on July 26, 1941, which number in any case would not exceed 25,000 and which number would not be subject to replacement.

3. The Government of the United States undertakes forthwith to remove the freezing restrictions which were placed on Japanese assets in the United States on July 26 and the Japanese Government agrees simultaneously to remove the freezing measures which it imposed in regard to American assets in Japan. Exports from each country would thereafter remain subject to the respective export control measures which each country may have in effect for reasons of national defense.

4. The Government of the United States undertakes forthwith to approach the British and the Dutch Governments with a view to those Governments' taking, on a basis of reciprocity with Japan, measures similar to those provided for in paragraph three above.

5. The Government of the United States would not look with disfavor upon the inauguration of conversations between the Government of China and the Government of Japan directed toward a peaceful settlement of their differences nor would the Government of the United States look with disfavor upon an armistice during the period of any such discussion. The fundamental interest of the Government of the United States in reference to any such discussions is simply that they be based upon and exemplify the fundamental principles of peace which constitute the central spirit of the current conversations between the Government of Japan and the Government of the United States.

   In case any such discussions are entered into between the Government of Japan and the Government of China, the Government of the United States is agreeable to such discussions taking place in the Philippine Islands, if so desired by both China and Japan.

6. It is understood that this *modus vivendi* is of a temporary nature and shall not remain in effect for a period longer than three months unless renewed by common agreement.

Hull's Final Offer

Never enthusiastic about the *modus vivendi,* Hull only gave passive support to the idea. When it was received coldly by Britain and China he decided to drop the plan. In its place, on November 26, he rejected Japan's Proposal B and offered a ten-point proposal that wiped out many concessions the United States had put forth in the preliminary conversations. The note he presented to Nomura was, on the major issues, largely uncompromising, though some of its lesser provisions were looked upon with favor by Japan. When presented with Hull's note, Japanese representatives in Washington were so dismayed that they were reluctant to send it to Tokyo.

Since Hull was fully aware that Proposal B was to be Japan's final offer, and since he was aware that the contents of his November 26 note were unacceptable to Japan on several critical issues, he was in effect terminating further discussion. While it technically was not an ultimatum, the uncompromising nature of Hull's note virtually amounted to a severance of diplomatic relations.

Oral Statement[5]
Handed by the Secretary of State
to the Japanese Ambassador (Nomura) on November 26, 1941

The representatives of the Government of the United States and of the Government of Japan have been carrying on during the past several months informal and exploratory conversations for the purpose of arriving at a settlement if possible of questions relating to the entire Pacific area based upon the principles of peace, law and order and fair dealing among nations. . . .

It is believed that in our discussions some progress has been made in reference to the general principles which constitute the basis of a peaceful settlement covering the entire Pacific area. Recently the Japanese Ambassador has stated that the Japanese Government is desirous of continuing the conversations directed toward a comprehensive and peaceful settlement in the Pacific area; that it would be helpful toward creating an atmosphere favorable to the successful outcome of the conversations if a temporary *modus vivendi* could be agreed upon to be in effect while the conversations looking to a peaceful settlement . . . were continuing. On November 20 the Japanese Ambassador communicated to the Secretary of State proposals in regard to temporary measures to be taken respectively by the Government of Japan and by the Government of the United States, which measures are understood to have been designed to accomplish the purposes above indicated.

The Government of the United States most earnestly desires to contribute to the promotion and maintenance of peace and stability in the Pacific area, and to afford every opportunity for the continuance of discussions with the Japanese Government directed toward working out a broad-gauge program of peace throughout the Pacific area. The proposals which were presented by the Japanese Ambassador . . . contain some features which, in the opinion of this Government, conflict with the fundamental principles which form a part of the general settlement under consideration and to which each Government has declared that it is committed. The Government of the United States believes that the adoption of such proposals would not be likely to contribute to the ultimate objectives of ensuring peace under law, order and justice in the Pacific area, and it suggests that further effort be made to resolve our divergences of views in regard to the practical application of the fundamental principles already mentioned.

With this object in view the Government of the United States offers for the consideration of the Japanese Government a plan of a broad but simple settlement covering the entire Pacific area as one practical exemplification of a program which this Government envisages as something to be worked out during our further conversations.

The plan therein suggested represents an effort to bridge the gap between our draft of June 21, 1941 and the Japanese draft of September 25 by making a new approach to the essential problems underlying a comprehensive Pacific settlement. This plan contains provisions dealing with the practical application of the fundamental principles which we have agreed in our conversations constitute the only sound basis for worthwhile international relations. We hope that in this way progress toward reaching a meeting of minds between our two Governments may be expedited.

Hull to Nomura, November 26, 1941[6]

Outline of Proposed Basis for Agreement
Between the United States and Japan

Section I
Draft Mutual Declaration of Policy
The Government of the United States and the Government of Japan both being solicitous for the peace of the Pacific affirm that their national policies are directed toward lasting and extensive peace throughout the Pacific area, that they have no territorial designs in that area, that they have no intention of threatening other countries or of using military force aggressively against any neighboring nation, and that, accordingly, in their national policies they will actively support and give practical application to the following fundamental principles upon which their relations with each other and with all other governments are based:
1. The principle of inviolability of territorial integrity and sovereignty of each and all nations.
2. The principle of non-interference in the internal affairs of other countries.
3. The principle of equality, including the equality of commercial opportunity and treatment.
4. The principle of reliance upon international cooperation and conciliation for the prevention and pacific settlement of controversies and

for improvement of international conditions by peaceful methods and processes.

The Government of Japan and the Government of the United States have agreed that toward eliminating chronic political instability, preventing recurrent economic collapse, and providing a basis for peace, they will actively support and practically apply the following principles in their economic relations with each other and with other nations and peoples:

1. The principle of non-discrimination in international commercial relations.
2. The principle of international economic cooperation and abolition of extreme nationalism as expressed in excessive trade restrictions.
3. The principle of non-discriminatory access by all nations to raw material supplies.
4. The principle of full protection of the interests of consuming countries and populations as regards the operation of international commodity agreements.
5. The principle of establishment of such institutions and arrangements of international finance as may lend aid to the essential enterprises and the continuous development of all countries and may permit payments through processes of trade consonant with the welfare of all countries.

Section II
Steps to be Taken by the Government of the United States
and by the Government of Japan

The Government of the United States and the Government of Japan propose to take steps as follows:

1. The Government of the United States and the Government of Japan will endeavor to conclude a multilateral non-aggression pact among the British Empire, China, Japan, the Netherlands, the Soviet Union, Thailand and the United States.
2. Both Governments will endeavor to conclude among the American, British, Chinese, Japanese, the Netherland and Thai Governments an agreement whereunder each of the Governments would pledge itself to respect the territorial integrity of French Indochina and, in the event that there should develop a threat to the territorial integrity of Indochina, to enter into immediate consultation with a view to taking such measures as may be deemed necessary and advisable to meet the threat in question. Such agreement would provide also that each of the Governments party to the agreement would not seek or accept preferential treatment in its trade or economic relations with Indochina and would use its influence to obtain for each of the signatories equality of treatment in trade and commerce with French Indochina.
3. The Government of Japan will withdraw all military, naval, air and police forces from China and from Indochina.

4. The Government of the United States and the Government of Japan will not support—militarily, politically, economically—any government or regime in China other than the national Government of the Republic of China with capital temporarily at Chungking.

5. Both Governments will endeavor to obtain the agreement of the British and other governments to give up extraterritorial rights in China, including rights and interests in and with regard to international settlements and concessions, and rights under the Boxer Protocol of 1901.

6. The Government of the United States and the Government of Japan will enter into negotiations for the conclusion between the United States and Japan of a trade agreement, based upon reciprocal most-favored-nation treatment and reduction of trade barriers by both countries, including an undertaking by the United States to bind raw silk on the free list.

7. The Government of the United States and the Government of Japan will, respectively, remove the freezing restrictions on Japanese funds in the United States and on American funds in Japan.

8. Both Governments will agree upon a plan for the stabilization of the dollar-yen rate, with the allocation of funds for this purpose, half to be supplied by Japan and half by the United States.

9. Both Governments will agree that no agreement which either has concluded with any third power or powers shall be interpreted by it in such a way as to conflict with the fundamental purpose of this agreement, the establishment and preservation of peace throughout the Pacific area.

10. Both Governments will use their influence to cause other governments to adhere to and to give practical application to the basic political and economic principles set forth in this agreement.

Were The Japanese Sincere?

In the years that followed the Pearl Harbor attack American propaganda depicted Japanese efforts at negotiation during 1941 as insincere and designed to keep the United States off balance. Special envoy Kurusu was described in "War Comes to America," a widely-shown World War II documentary, as flashing "his toothy smile" as he spoke of peace. Cordell Hull, in the same film, dismissed the note delivered to him by Nomura and Kurusu on December 7, while the bombs were falling in Hawaii, as a monstrous falsehood. Even the timing of the note's delivery, *after* the bombing attack had begun, was cited as an indication of Japanese treachery.

Were the Japanese sincere in their efforts to settle differences with the United States diplomatically? Or were they simply dragging out discussions until the military was ready to strike? Here, culled from a multitude of dispatches released by Congress during the Pearl Harbor Hearings immediately after the war, are representative samples of Japanese notes to and from their own diplomats that were not intended for public release, though they were intercepted and decoded by American intelligence, and therefore can be read as indicative of Japanese sincerity, or lack of it.

Intercepted Japanese Notes[7]

Canton to Tokyo   July 14, 1941

. . . The recent general mobilization order expressed the irrevocable resolution of Japan to put an end to Anglo-American assistance in thwarting her natural expansion and her indomitable intention to carry this out, if possible, with the backing of the Axis but, if necessary, alone. . . .

Tokyo to Berlin   July 19, 1941

The Cabinet shake up [ouster of Foreign Minister Matsuoka] was necessary to expedite matters in connection with National affairs and has no further significance. Japan's foreign policy will not be changed and she will remain faithful to the principles of the Tripartite Pact.

Tokyo to Washington   July 31, 1941

. . . Commercial and economic relations between Japan and third countries, led by England and the United States, are gradually becoming so horribly strained that we cannot endure it much longer. Consequently, our Empire, to save its very life, must take measures to secure the raw materials of the South Seas. Our Empire must immediately take steps to break asunder this ever-strengthening chain of encirclement which is being woven under the guidance and with the participation of England and the United States, acting like a cunning dragon seemingly asleep. That is why we decided to obtain military bases in French Indo-China and to have our troops occupy that territory. . . .

Tokyo to Washington   October 21, 1941

. . . The new cabinet [under Tojo] differs in no way from the former one in its sincere desire to adjust Japanese-United States relations on a fair basis. Our country has said practically all she can say in the way of expressing of opinions and setting forth our stands. We feel that we have now reached a point where no further positive action can be taken by us except to urge the United States to reconsider her views.

We urge, therefore, that, choosing an opportune moment, either you [Nomura] or Wakasugi [Nomura's second-in-command] let it be known to the United States by indirection that our country is not in a position to spend much more time discussing this matter. Please continue the talks, emphasizing our desire for a formal United States counter-proposal to our proposal of 25 September.

Tokyo to Washington   November 4, 1941

. . . Conditions both within and without our Empire are so tense that no longer is procrastination possible, yet in our sincerity to maintain pacific relationships between the Empire of Japan and the United States of America, we have decided, as a result of these deliberations, to gamble once more on the continuance of the parleys, but this is our last effort. Both in name and spirit this counter-proposal of ours is, indeed, the last. I want you to know that. If through it we do not reach a quick accord, I am sorry to say the talks will certainly be ruptured. Then, indeed, will relations between our two nations be on the brink of chaos. I mean that the success or failure of the pending discussions will have an immense effect on the destiny of the Empire of Japan. In fact, we gambled the fate of our land on the throw of this die.

When the Japanese-American meetings began, who would have ever dreamt that they would drag out so long? Hoping that we could fast come to some understanding, we have already gone far out of our way and yielded and yielded. The United States does not appreciate this, but through thick and thin sticks to the selfsame propositions she made to start with. Those of our people and of our officials who suspect the sincerity of the Americans are far from few. Bearing all kinds of humiliating things, our Government has repeatedly stated its sincerity and gone far, yes, too far, in giving in to them. There is just one reason why we do this—to maintain peace in the Pacific. . . . This time we are making our last possible bargain, and I hope that we can thus settle all our troubles with the United States peaceably.

Tokyo to Washington   November 5, 1941

. . . As stated in my previous message, this is the Imperial Government's final step. Time is becoming exceedingly short and the situation very critical. Absolutely no delays can be permitted. Please bear this in mind and do your best. . . .

We wish to avoid giving them the impression that there is a time limit or that this proposal is to be taken as an ultimatum. In a friendly manner, show them that we are very anxious to have them accept our proposal. . . .

Tokyo to Washington   November 5, 1941

(Of utmost secrecy)

Because of various circumstances, it is absolutely necessary that all arrangements for the signing of this agreement (Proposal A or B) be completed by the 25th of this month. I realize that this is a difficult order, but under the circumstances it is an unavoidable one. Please understand this thoroughly and tackle the problem of saving the Japanese-U. S. relations from falling into a chaotic condition. Do so with great determination and with unstinted effort, I beg of you.

This information is to be kept strictly to yourself only.

Tokyo to Washington   November 6, 1941

The reason why we are sending Ambassador KURUSU to you so quickly is, in addition to what I have already wired you, to show our Empire's sincerity in the negotiations soon to follow. As I wired you before, he brings with him no new instruction in addition to the ones I have already sent you. I wish him, however, to communicate to you first hand as best he may, the exact situation here in Japan, and now that we are on the last lap of these negotiations, I do hope that he can help you in unravelling this bewildering maze and through cooperation lead to a solution, and that right soon. To make it sound good, we are telling the public that he is coming to help you quickly compose the unhappy relations between the two nations. We have explained all this fully to the British and American Ambassadors here in Tokyo, and Ambassador KURUSU himself had a heart-to-heart talk with the American Ambassador here before he left, and both Ambassadors fully understand why he is making the trip. . . .

Tokyo to Hongkong   November 14, 1941

Though the Imperial Government hopes for great things from the Japanese-American negotiations, they do not permit optimism for the future. Should the negotiations collapse, the international situation in which the Empire will find herself will be one of tremendous crisis. Accompanying this, the Empires's foreign policy as it has been decided by the cabinet, insofar as it pertains to China, is:

   a. We will completely destroy British and American power in China.
   b. We will take over all enemy concessions and enemy important rights and interests (customs and minerals, etc.) in China.
   c. We will take over all rights and interests owned by enemy powers, even though they might have connections with the new Chinese government, should it become necessary. . . .

Tokyo to Washington   November 22, 1941

[Foreign Minister Shigenori Togo extended the cutoff date to November 29.] . . . After that things are automatically going to happen.

Washington to Tokyo   November 30, 1941

TransPacific Radio Telephone

. . . Kurusu: [In Washington] "Are the Japanese-American negotiations to continue?"

Yamamoto [Japanese foreign office, American bureau]: "Yes."

Kurusu: "You were very urgent about them before, weren't you: but now
you want them to stretch out. We will need your help. Both the Premier and the Foreign Minister will need to change the tone of their
speeches! Do you understand? Please all use more discretion. . . . "

Notes

1. *Pearl Harbor Attack,* part 14, 1061–1062.
2. *Ibid.,* part 12, 94–96.
3. *Foreign Relations: Japan,* II, 755–756.
4. *Pearl Harbor Attack,* part 14, 1113–1115.
5. *Foreign Relations: Japan,* II, 766–768.
6. *Ibid,* II, 768–770.
7. *Pearl Harbor Attack,* part 12, exhibit 1. [Japanese dispatches, to or from envoys abroad, intercepted by the United States prior to the Pearl Harbor attack.]

IX

AN END TO DIPLOMATIC
CONVERSATIONS

By December 6, 1941, the military situation between Japan and the United States was at the crisis stage. Large Japanese troopship concentrations were reported off Indochina, Japanese warships cruised the waters north of Luzon in the Philippines, and a Japanese task force made final, but unobserved, preparations for the attack on Pearl Harbor. For their part, American pilots, under nominal Chinese command, guarded the Burma Road. High officials in the Roosevelt Administration expected a suspension of diplomatic relations between the two nations to occur shortly.

The Japanese fleet selected to strike Hawaii had sailed from Japan early on the morning of November 26 (the 25th in Washington). While officials in Washington were aware that war was imminent, expert opinion in Washington had predicted that a Japanese attack would come in the Far East, not Hawaii. Military commanders throughout the Pacific were on alert, yet the Japanese strike force reached its launch point north of Hawaii without detection.

Most Americans still thought the major crisis was in the Atlantic, where German submarines had attacked American warships and freighters with a significant loss of life. To them, the Japanese threat seemed somewhat remote.

The blow that fell at Pearl Harbor on December 7 shocked and surprised the American public.

Roosevelt Appeals To The Emperor

In an eleventh-hour effort, President Roosevelt appealed directly to Emperor Hirohito, hoping the Emperor's personal influence would stave off the headlong rush toward war. Roosevelt's appeal was apparently doomed to failure. Delivery of his plea was delayed by Japanese authorities until after midnight, Tokyo time, on December 8. By then the Emperor had retired for the night and Foreign Minister Shigenori Togo did not reach him with news of the President's plea until 3:00 a.m. Far to the east, the first flights of Japanese planes were already nearing Pearl Harbor.

President Roosevelt to Emperor Hirohito of Japan[1]

Washington, December 6, 1941

Almost a century ago the President of the United States addressed to the Emperor of Japan a message extending an offer of friendship of the people of the United States to the people of Japan. That offer was accepted, and in the long period of unbroken peace and friendship which has followed, our respective nations, through the virtues of their peoples and the wisdom of their rulers have prospered and have substantially helped humanity.

Only in situations of extraordinary importance to our two countries need I address to Your Majesty messages on matters of state. I feel I should now so address you because of the deep and far reaching emergency which appears to be in formation.

Developments are occurring in the Pacific area which threaten to deprive each of our nations and all humanity of the beneficial influence of the long peace between our two countries. These developments contain tragic possibilities.

The people of the United States, believing in peace and in the right of nations to live and let live, have eagerly watched the conversations between our two governments during these past months. We have hoped for a termination of the present conflict between Japan and China. We have hoped that a peace of the Pacific could be consummated in such a way that nationalities of many diverse peoples could exist side by side without fear of invasion; that unbearable burdens of armaments could be lifted for them all; and that all peoples would resume commerce without discrimination against or in favor of any nation.

I am certain it will be clear to Your Majesty as it is to me, that in seeking these great objectives both Japan and the United States should agree to eliminate any form of military threat. . . .

More than a year ago Your Majesty's Government concluded an agreement with the Vichy Government by which five or six thousand

Japanese troops were permitted to enter into Northern French Indo-China for protection of Japanese troops which were operating against China further north. And this Spring and Summer the Vichy Government permitted further Japanese military forces to enter into Southern French Indo-China for the common defense of French Indo-China. I think I am correct in saying that no attack has been made upon Indo-China, nor that any has been contemplated.

During the past few weeks it has become clear to the world that Japanese military, naval, and air forces have been sent to Southern Indo-China in such large numbers as to create a reasonable doubt on the part of other nations that this continuing concentration in Indo-China is not defensive in its character.

Because these continuing concentrations in Indo-China have reached large proportions and because they extend now to the southeast and southwest corners of the Peninsula, it is only reasonable that the people of the Philippines, of the hundreds of islands of the East Indies, of Malaya and of Thailand itself are asking themselves whether these forces of Japan are preparing or intending to make attack in one or more of these many directions.

I am sure that Your Majesty will understand that the fear of all these peoples is a legitimate fear in as much as it involves their peace and their national existence. I am sure that Your Majesty will understand why the people of the United States in such large numbers look askance at the establishment of military, naval, and air bases manned and equipped so greatly as to constitute armed forces capable of measures of offense.

It is clear that a continuance of such a situation is unthinkable.

None of the peoples whom I have spoken of above can sit either indefinitely or permanently on a keg of dynamite.

There is absolutely no thought on the part of the United States of invading Indo-China if every Japanese soldier or sailor were to be withdrawn therefrom.

I think that we can obtain the same assurances from the Government of the East Indies, the Government of Malaya, and the Government of Thailand. I would even undertake to ask for the same assurance on the part of the Government of China. Thus a withdrawal of the Japanese forces from Indo-China would result in the assurance of peace throughout the whole of the South Pacific area.

I address myself to Your Majesty at this moment in the fervent hope that Your Majesty may, as I am doing, give thought in this definite emergency to ways of dispelling the dark clouds. I am confident that both of us, for the sake of peoples not only of our own great countries but for the sake of humanity in neighboring territories, have a sacred duty to restore traditional amity and prevent further death and destruction in the world.

Franklin D. Roosevelt

Japan Ends Diplomatic Negotiations

Throughout the day and night of December 6, 1941, American decoding experts were at work on a lengthy message they were then intercepting. The document, in fourteen parts, included the reply of the Japanese government to the American ten-point proposal of November 26 but, for the first time, contained no counterproposal. Ambassador Nomura and Special Envoy Kurusu were instructed to deliver it to Secretary Hull and/or President Roosevelt on December 7 at 1:00 p.m., Washington time. (The Japanese fleet within an hour after the delivery would be surprising United States forces at Pearl Harbor.) However, the Japanese Embassy had difficulty preparing the formal copy of the note for delivery to Hull and they did not arrive until 1:45. By the time they were received, Secretary Hull knew of the raid on Pearl Harbor, although both Nomura and Kurusu were apparently unaware that it had occurred.

The attack at Pearl Harbor stunned the American people and united them with the Allied cause. They were determined to punish the Japanese, believing that they had struck while peace negotiations were still being conducted. The American government, however, despite President Roosevelt's statement to Congress on December 8 that the Japanese note which had been delivered on Sunday contained no hint of war or armed attack, was well aware that Japanese action was imminent.

When the fourteen-part message was shown to the President after being decoded on December 6 he reportedly said, in substance: "This means war!" But the public was unaware of what the government had known all along and overwhelmingly accepted the position put forth by the President in his report to Congress the day after the raid: "Yesterday, December 7, 1941—a date which will live in infamy—the United States of America was suddenly and deliberately attacked by naval and air forces of the Empire of Japan." The United States was in World War II.

Memorandum [2]
Handed by the Japanese Ambassador (Nomura)
to the Secretary of State at 2:20 P. M. on December 7, 1941

1. The Government of Japan, prompted by a genuine desire to come to an amicable understanding with the Government of the United States in order that the two countries by their joint efforts may secure the

peace of the Pacific Area and thereby contribute toward the realization of world peace, has continued negotiations with the utmost sincerity since April last with the Government of the United States regarding the adjustment and advancement of Japanese-American relations and the stabilization of the Pacific Area.

The Japanese Government has the honor to state frankly its views concerning the claims the American Government has persistently maintained as well as the measures the United States and Great Britain have taken toward Japan during these eight months.

2. It is the immutable policy of the Japanese Government to insure the stability of East Asia and to promote world peace and thereby to enable all nations to find each its proper place in the world.

Ever since the China Affair broke out owing to the failure on the part of China to comprehend Japan's true intentions, the Japanese Government has striven for the restoration of peace and it has consistently exerted its best efforts to prevent the extension of war-like disturbances. It was also to that end that in September last year Japan concluded the Tripartite Pact with Germany and Italy.

However, both the United States and Great Britain have resorted to every possible measure to assist the Chungking regime so as to obstruct the establishment of a general peace between Japan and China, interfering with Japan's constructive endeavors toward the stabilization of East Asia. Exerting pressure on the Netherlands East Indies, or menacing French Indo-China, they have attempted to frustrate Japan's aspiration to the ideal of common prosperity in cooperation with these regions. Furthermore, when Japan in accordance with its protocol with France took measures of joint defence of French Indo-China, both American and British Governments wilfully misinterpreting it as a threat to their own possessions, and inducing the Netherlands Government to follow suit, they enforced the assets freezing order, thus severing economic relations with Japan. While manifesting thus an obviously hostile attitude, these countries have strengthened their military preparations perfecting an encirclement of Japan, and have brought about a situation which endangers the very existence of the Empire. . . .

3. . . . As regards China, the Japanese Government, while expressing its readiness to accept the offer of the President of the United States to act as "introducer" of peace between Japan and China as was previously suggested, asked for an undertaking on the part of the United States to do nothing prejudicial to the restoration of Sino-Japanese peace when the two parties have commenced direct negotiation.

The American Government not only rejected the above-mentioned new proposal, but made known its intention to continue its aid to Chiang Kai-Shek; and in spite of its suggestion mentioned above, withdrew the offer of the President to act as so-called "introducer" of peace between Japan and China, pleading that time was not yet ripe for it. Finally on November 26th, in an attitude to impose upon the Japanese Government those principles it has persistently maintained, the American Government made a proposal totally ignoring Japanese claims, which is a source of profound regret to the Japanese Government.

4. From the beginning of the present negotiations the Japanese Government has always maintained an attitude of fairness and moderation, and did its best to reach a settlement, for which it made all possible concessions often in spite of great difficulties. . . .

It is presumed that the spirit of conciliation exhibited to the utmost degree by the Japanese Government in all these matters is fully appreciated by the American Government.

On the other hand, the American Government, always holding fast to theories in disregard of realities, and refusing to yield an inch on its impractical principles, caused undue delay in the negotiation. It is difficult to understand this attitude of the American Government and the Japanese Government desires to call the attention of the American Government especially to the following points:

a. The American Government advocates in the name of world peace those principles favorable to it and urges upon the Japanese Government the acceptance thereof. The peace of the world may be brought about only by discovering a mutually acceptable formula through recognition of the reality of the situation and mutual appreciation of one another's position. An attitude such as ignores realities and imposes one's selfish views upon others will scarcely serve the purpose of facilitating the consummation of negotiations. Of the various principles put forward by the American Government as a basis of the Japanese-American Agreement, there are some which the Japanese Government is ready to accept in principle, but in view of the world's actual conditions, it seems only a utopian ideal on the part of the American Government to attempt to force their immediate adoption. . . .

b. . . . The American Government, obsessed with its own views and opinions, may be said to be scheming for the extension of the war. While it seeks, on the one hand, to secure its rear by stabilizing the Pacific Area, it is engaged, on the other hand, in aiding Great Britain and preparing to attack, in the name of self-defense, Germany and Italy, two Powers that are striving to establish a new order in Europe. Such a policy is totally at variance with the many principles upon which the American Government proposes to found the stability of the Pacific Area through peaceful means.

c. Whereas the American Government, under the principles it rigidly upholds, objects to settle international issues through military pressure, it is exercising in conjunction with Great Britain and other nations pressure by economic power. Recourse to such pressure as a means of dealing with international relations should be condemned as it is at times more inhumane than military pressure.

d. It is impossible not to reach the conclusion that the American Government desires to maintain and strengthen, in coalition with Great Britain and other Powers, its dominant position it has hitherto occupied not only in China but in other areas of East Asia. It is a fact of history that the countries of East Asia for the past hundred years or more have been compelled to observe the *status quo* under the Anglo-American policy of imperialistic exploitation and to sacrifice themselves to the prosperity of the two nations. The Japanese Government cannot tolerate the perpetuation of such a situation since it directly runs counter to Japan's fundamental policy to enable all nations to enjoy each its proper place in the world.

The stipulation proposed by the American Government relative to French Indo-China is a good exemplification of the above-mentioned American policy. Thus the six countries—Japan, the United States, Great Britain, the Netherlands, China and Thailand—excepting France, should undertake among themselves to respect the territorial integrity and sovereignty of French Indo-China and equality of treatment in trade and commerce would be tantamount to placing that territory under the joint guarantee of the Governments of those six countries. Apart from the fact that such a proposal totally ignores the position of France, it is unacceptable to the Japanese Government in that such an arrangement cannot but be considered as an extension to French Indo-China of a system similar to the Nine Power Treaty structure which is the chief factor responsible for the present predicament of East Asia.

e. All the items demanded of Japan by the American Government regarding China such as the wholesale evacuation of troops or unconditional application of the principle of non-discrimination in international commerce ignored the actual conditions of China, and are calculated to destroy Japan's position as the stabilizing factor of East Asia. The attitude of the American Government in demanding Japan not to support militarily, politically or economically any regime other than the regime at Chungking, disregarding thereby the existence of the Nanking Government, shatters the very basis of the present negotiation. This demand of the American Government falling, as it does, in line with its above-mentioned refusal to cease from aiding the Chungking regime, demonstrates clearly the intention of the American Gov-

ernment to obstruct the restoration of normal relations between
Japan and China and the return of peace to East Asia.

5. In brief, the American proposal contains certain acceptable items such
as those concerning commerce, including the conclusion of a trade
agreement, mutual removal of the freezing restrictions, and stabilization of yen and dollar exchange, or the abolition of extraterritorial
rights in China. On the other hand, however, the proposal in question
ignores Japan's sacrifices in the four years of the China Affair, men-
aces the Empire's existence itself and disparages its honour and prestige. Therefore, viewed in its entirety, the Japanese Government
regrets that it cannot accept the proposal as a basis of negotiation.

6. The Japanese Government, in its desire for an early conclusion of the
negotiation, proposed simultaneously with the conclusion of the Japanese-American negotiation, agreements to be signed with Great Britain and other interested countries. The proposal was accepted by the
American Government. However, since the American Government
has made the proposal of November 26th as a result of frequent consultation with Great Britain, Australia, the Netherlands and
Chungking, and presumably by catering to the wishes of the
Chungking regime in the questions of China, it must be concluded
that all these countries are at one with the United States in ignoring
Japan's position.

7. Obviously, it is the intention of the American Government to conspire
with Great Britain and other countries to obstruct Japan's efforts toward the establishment of peace through the creation of a new order
in East Asia, and especially to preserve Anglo-American rights and
interests by keeping Japan and China at war. This intention has been
revealed clearly during the course of the present negotiation. Thus,
the earnest hope of the Japanese Government to adjust Japanese-
American relations and to preserve and promote the peace of the
Pacific through cooperation with the American Government has finally been lost.

The Japanese Government regrets to have to notify hereby the American Government that in view of the attitude of the American Government
it cannot but consider that it is impossible to reach an agreement through
further negotiations.

Notes

1. *Foreign Relations: Japan*, II, 784–786.
2. *Ibid.*, II, 787–792.

CHRONOLOGY

May 1, 1898	U. S. Victory at Manila
November 13, 1899	Hay's First Open Door Note to Japan
July 3, 1900	Hay's Second Open Door Note to Japan
July 29, 1905	Taft-Katsura Agreement
November 30, 1908	Root-Takahira Agreement
January, 1915	Japan's Twenty-One Demands on China
November 2, 1917	Lansing-Ishii Agreement
December 13, 1921	Four-Power Treaty (Washington Conference)
February 6, 1922	Five-Power and Nine-Power Treaties (Washington Conference)
August 27, 1928	Kellogg-Briand Pact
September 18, 1931	"Manchurian Incident" near Mukden
January 7, 1932	Stimson Doctrine
March 27, 1933	Japan Quits the League
November 25, 1936	Anti-Comintern Pact
July 7, 1937	Clash at the Marco Polo Bridge: Sino-Japanese War Begins
October 5, 1937	Roosevelt's Quarantine Speech

December 12, 1937	Japan Sinks the *Panay*
July 26, 1939	U. S. Abrogates 1911 Commercial Treaty with Japan
August 23, 1939	Hitler-Stalin Nonaggression Pact
September 1, 1939	Germany Invades Poland
July, 1940	Export Controls Imposed on U. S. Trade with Japan
September, 1940	Japan Occupies Northern Indochina
September 27, 1940	Axis Pact Signed
April 13, 1941	Japan-Soviet Neutrality Pact
April-June, 1941	U. S. and Japan Exchange Draft Treaties
June 22, 1941	Germany Attacks Russia
July 2, 1941	Japanese Imperial Conference Confirms Move to South
July 23, 1941	Japan Occupies Southern Indochina
July 26, 1941	Roosevelt Freezes All Japanese Assets in U. S.
August 1, 1941	Roosevelt Embargoes Sale of Petroleum to Japan
August 9, 1941	Roosevelt and Churchill Meet, Oppose Japanese Expansion
August 17, 1941	Roosevelt Warns Japan
September 6, 1941	Japan Sets October Deadline for Negotiations
October 16, 1941	Konoye Cabinet Resigns, Tojo New Premier
October 23, 1941	Japan Decides to Continue Negotiations into November
November 6, 1961	Stark-Marshall Memorandum
November 7, 1941	Japanese Set Date for Pearl Harbor Attack Proposal A Presented to U. S.

November 15, 1941	Special Envoy Kurusu Arrives in Washington
November 20, 1941	Proposal B Presented to U. S.
November 25, 1941	Japanese Carriers Leave for Pearl Harbor Attack
November 26, 1941	Hull Rejects Proposal B
November 27, 1941	U. S. Sends War Warning to Pearl Harbor and Other Bases
November 29, 1941	Japanese Deadline for Successful Negotiations
December 1, 1941	Emperor Approves War Plans
December 6, 1941	Roosevelt Appeals to the Emperor Japan's Fourteen-Part Message Decoded by U. S.
December 7, 1941	Attack on Pearl Harbor

DIRECTORY

(Only officials referred to in the introductions or documents are listed.)

American Secretaries of State

John Hay (1898–1905), under William McKinley and Theodore Roosevelt
Elihu Root (1905–1909, under Theodore Roosevelt
Robert Lansing (1915–1920), under Woodrow Wilson
Charles Evans Hughes (1921–1925), under Warren Harding and Calvin
    Coolidge
Frank B. Kellogg (1925–1929), under Calvin Coolidge
Henry L. Stimson (1929–1933), under Herbert Hoover
Cordell Hull (1933–1944), under Franklin Roosevelt

American Ambassadors to Japan

William C. Forbes (1930–1932)
Joseph C. Grew (1932–1941)

Japanese Prime Ministers

Count Taro Katsura (1905)
Prince Fumimaro Konoye (1940–1941)
Hideki Tojo (1941)

Japanese Foreign Ministers

Viscount Siuzo Aoki (1899)
Baron Kijuro Shidehara (1929–1931)
Koki Hirota (1933–1936)
Hachiro Arita (1936–1937)
Koki Hirota (1937–1938)
Hachiro Arita (1938–1939)
Kichisaburo Nomura (1939–1940)
Hachiro Arita (1940)
Yosuke Matsuoka (1940–1941)
Teijiro Toyoda (1941)
Shigenori Togo (1941–1942)

Japanese Ambassadors to the United States

Kogoro Takahira (1908)
Kikujiro Ishii (1917)
Katsuji Debuchi (1928–1934)
Hirosi Saito (1934–1938)
Kensuke Horinouchi (1938–1940)
Kichisaburo Nomura (1941)

Miscellaneous Officials

Chiang Kai-shek (leader of Kuomintang Party in China, head of Nationalist government from late 1920s on)

Wang Ching-wei (head of pro-Japanese government for China, at Nanking, recognized in 1940)

Nelson Johnson (American Minister and Ambassador to China, 1930–1941)

Saburo Kurusu (Special Japanese Envoy to the U. S., November–December, 1941)

FURTHER READINGS

The amount of library material available on the coming of war with Japan is truly staggering. In the first forty-nine years following the Japanese attack on Pearl Harbor nearly fifty scholarly works on that subject had appeared with the name "Pearl Harbor" in the title or subtitle, and that was before the avalanche of publications issued commemorating the fiftieth anniversary of the raid. To help those who wish to read further on the war's origins without getting lost in the shelves of books that now abound, the following list of suggested readings may be helpful.

Four traditional diplomatic histories of the United States stand out as overall surveys of American foreign policy during the period 1899–1941. Old but still important because of his interpretation of American imperialism at the turn of the century is Samuel Flagg Bemis, *A Diplomatic History of the United States* (1965). Thomas A. Bailey, *A Diplomatic History of the American People* (1980) is the long-established text in that field. Two more recent surveys are especially useful: Walter LaFeber, *The American Age: United States Foreign Policy at Home and Abroad since 1750* (1989) and Thomas G. Paterson et al, *American Foreign Policy* (1991).

For volumes covering American relations with China and Japan over a long period of time, see Warren I. Cohen, *America's Response to China* (1980); Charles E. Neu, *The Troubled Encounter: The United States and Japan* (1975); William L. Neumann, *America Encounters Japan: From Perry to MacArthur* (1963); and Edwin O. Reischauer, *The United States and Japan* (1957).

Long recognized as a major contribution to an understanding of late nineteenth and early twentieth century American policy in the Far East is A. Whitney Griswold, *The Far Eastern Policy of the United States* (1938), which is still good on the origins of the Open Door, though dated in light of subsequent scholarship. Griswold should be read in conjunction with Jerry Israel, *Progressivism and the Open Door: America and China, 1905–1921* (1971); George Kennan, *American Diplomacy, 1900–1950* (1951); and William A. Williams, *The Tragedy of American Diplomacy* (1962).

Relations with Japan during the period 1899–1921 are chronicled by Tyler Dennett, *Roosevelt and the Russo-Japanese War* (1925); Raymond A. Esthus, *Theodore Roosevelt and Japan* (1966); Akira Iriye, *Pacific Estrangement: Japanese and American Expansion, 1897–1911* (1972); and Charles E. Neu, *An Uncertain Friendship: Theodore Roosevelt and Japan, 1906–1909* (1967).

On Woodrow Wilson's Far Eastern policy, see Burton F. Beers, *Vain Endeavor: Robert Lansing's Attempt to end the American-Japanese Rivalry* (1962); Roy W. Curry, *Woodrow Wilson and Far Eastern Policy, 1913–1921* (1957); and Roger Dingman, *Power in the Pacific: The Origins of Naval Arms Limitation, 1914–1922* (1976).

The international negotiations of the Republican era are found in Thomas H. Buckley, *The United States and the Washington Conference, 1921–1922* (1970); Richard D. Burns and Edward M. Bennett, eds., *Diplomats in Crisis: United States-Chinese-Japanese Relations, 1919–1931* (1974); Warren I. Cohen, *Empire Without Tears: America's Foreign Relations, 1921–1933* (1987); L. Ethan Ellis, *Republican Foreign Policy, 1921–1933* (1968); Robert H. Ferrell, *Peace in Their Time: Origins of the Kellogg-Briand Pact* (1952); Stephen Pelz, *The Race to Pearl Harbor* (1974); and Gerald E. Wheeler, *Prelude to Pearl Harbor: The United States Navy and the Far East, 1921–1931* (1963).

The Manchurian Incident is discussed in detail in Robert H. Ferrell, *American Diplomacy in the Great Depression: Hoover-Stimson Foreign Policy, 1929–1933* (1957); Armin Rappoport, *Henry L. Stimson and Japan, 1931–1933* (1963); Henry L. Stimson and McGeorge Bundy, *On Active Service in Peace and War* (1948); Christopher Thorne, *The Limits of Foreign Policy* (1972); and Takehiko Yoshihashi, *Conspiracy at Mukden: The Rise of the Japanese Military* (1963).

Much has been written on the foreign policy of Franklin Roosevelt, but the best one volume work is Robert Dallek, *Franklin D. Roosevelt and American Foreign Policy, 1933–1945* (1979). Other examinations of FDR's policy toward Japan are Irvine H. Anderson, The *Standard-Vacuum Oil Company and United States East Asia Policy, 1933–1941* (1975); Dorothy Borg, *The United States and the Far Eastern Crisis, 1933–1938* (1964); Dorothy Borg and Shumpei Okamoto, eds., *Pearl Harbor as History: Japanese-American Relations, 1931–1941* (1973); Joseph C. Grew, *Ten Years in Japan* (1944); James H. Herzog, *Closing the Open Door: American-Japanese Diplomatic Negotiations, 1936–1941* (1973); Akira Iriye, *The Origins of the Second World War in Asia and the Pacific* (1987); David J. Lu, *From the Marco Polo Bridge to Pearl Harbor* (1961); and Jonathan G. Utley, *Going to War with Japan, 1937–1941* (1985). Two works dealing specifically with the *Panay* crisis have almost identical titles: Manny T. Koginos, *The Panay Incident: Prelude to War* (1967); and Hamilton D. Perry, *The Panay Incident: Prelude to Pearl Harbor* (1969).

Japan's relations with Germany and Russia are explored in Paul W. Schroeder, *The Axis Alliance and Japanese-American Relations, 1941* (1958); and James W. Morley, ed., *Deterrent Diplomacy: Japan, Germany, and the U. S. S. R., 1935–1940* (1976).

The period immediately prior to the outbreak of war has naturally received the greatest attention. Of particularly important value are Robert J. C. Butow, *Tojo and the Coming of the War* (1961) and *The John Doe Associates: Backdoor Diplomacy for Peace, 1941* (1974); Ladislas Farago, *The Broken Seal* (1967); Herbert Feis, *The Road to Pearl Harbor* (1950); Nobutaka Ike, *Japan's Decision for War: Records of the 1941 Policy Conferences* (1967); Edwin T. Layton, *And I Was There* (1985); James W. Morley, ed., *The Fateful Choice: Japan's Advance into Southeast Asia, 1939–1941* (1980); Gordon Prange, *At Dawn We Slept* (1981); Bruce Russett, *No Clear and Present Danger* (1972); John Toland, *Infamy: Pearl Harbor and Its Aftermath* (1982); and Roberta Wohlstetter, *Pearl Harbor: Warning and Decision* (1962).

Most of the relevant documents quoted in the text are to be found in two main State Department publications. See U. S. Department of State, *Foreign Relations of the United States: Japan: 1931–1941* (1943), 2 Vols., and *Foreign Relations of the United States* for the appropriate year. In addition, much of the material that was not available to the public during the war was subsequently published in U. S. Congress Joint Committee on the Investigation of the Pearl Harbor Attack, *Pearl Harbor Attack: Hearings Before the Joint Committee...* 39 parts (1946).

Finally, for those who wish to read the scathing criticisms made by an earlier generation of Franklin Roosevelt's detractors,